Cambridge Handbooks for Teachers
GENERAL EDITOR: PROFESSOR J. W. ADAMSON

CITIZENSHIP
AND THE SCHOOL

CITIZENSHIP
AND THE SCHOOL

BY

P. B. SHOWAN, M.A.

Lecturer in Education in University of London,
King's College

CAMBRIDGE
AT THE UNIVERSITY PRESS
1923

CAMBRIDGE UNIVERSITY PRESS
Cambridge, New York, Melbourne, Madrid, Cape Town,
Singapore, São Paulo, Delhi, Mexico City

Cambridge University Press
The Edinburgh Building, Cambridge CB2 8RU, UK

Published in the United States of America by Cambridge University Press, New York

www.cambridge.org
Information on this title: www.cambridge.org/9781107623156

First published 1923
First paperback edition 2013

A catalogue record for this publication is available from the British Library

ISBN 978-1-107-62315-6 Paperback

GENERAL EDITOR'S PREFACE

THE enthusiastic reformer of society desires to throw many novel tasks upon the school, whether those tasks have any vital relation or not to the purposes for which schools exist. Men are not absolutely agreed as to what those purposes are; yet probably all would admit that, either as a primary or a secondary purpose, the making of good citizens (as distinct from good partisans) is one of the aims which schools should have in view. The circumstances of our time make that particular aim an obvious one for an institution so public as the school.

This book does not propose the intrusion of a new study into a curriculum already crowded, if not over-crowded. It describes, from the stand-point of the form-master, or form-mistress, not a new "subject" but an attitude towards studies whose right to appear in a school course, whether elementary or secondary, has long been recognized. Like its fellows in the present series, it is intended to assist school-room practice, not to present a purely theoretical discussion, though of course principles are by no means forgotten. The actual class-room is always present to the mind of the author, who knows from his own experience that his recommendations are feasible in schools where conditions are in no sense exceptional or especially favourable to teaching citizenship in a way both practical and interesting.

J. W. A.

PREFACE

THE following pages embody an attempt to outline a course of civic instruction based on the belief that the surest foundation for English political and civic education is a knowledge of England and the English people. The purpose of the book is three-fold: firstly, to emphasize the urgent need for civic instruction in English schools; secondly, to discuss and define the content of the subject suitable for school purposes; and thirdly, to outline a method by which adequate and stimulating civic instruction can be given in schools through the media of history and its allied studies without expense and with the least possible modification of existing syllabuses. It will be seen that the course gives pupils a sound body of knowledge, and affords them training which can no longer be denied a place in schools even if it displaces some matter which is taught at present.

Naturally 'many teachers, many methods'; but once the need for civic instruction is recognized and its claims accepted, teachers themselves will see to it that the teaching is developed and improved. The writer will be satisfied if this book helps to point out the way, and brings nearer the time when in all English schools the principles of citizenship, the rights and duties of citizens, and the elements of political economy are taught in such a way as to inculcate a respect for our national institutions, a desire and an aptitude for public and social service in after-life, and an abiding love for England.

P. B. S.

LONDON
August, 1923

CONTENTS

PART I

INTRODUCTORY

PART II

A SCHEME OF CIVIC INSTRUCTION BASED ON HISTORY, SHOWING THE FUNCTION OF HISTORY IN THE TEACHING OF CIVICS

PART III

SOME ECONOMIC ASPECTS OF SCHOOL GEOGRAPHY

PART IV

TRAINING IN SELF-GOVERNMENT

PART I

INTRODUCTORY

"No more vital truth was ever uttered than that freedom and free institutions cannot long be maintained by any people who do not understand the nature of their own Government."
WOODROW WILSON.

"The road to ruin for an ignorant and selfish democracy is far shorter than for any other kind of misgovernment; the fall is greater and the ruin more complete. There is no builder of the common good who builds so nobly and securely as a wise democracy; and there are no hands which destroy so helplessly as the hands of the many."
Sir HENRY JONES.

CHAPTER I

THE NEED FOR CIVIC INSTRUCTION

THE need for instruction in the principles of citizenship and the rights and obligations of citizens was never more urgent than it is to-day.

Years ago, when the franchise was limited and political parties more or less clearly defined, popular ignorance of civics was deplorable; but to-day, when democracy is complete and fully conscious of its powers, it is essential to our political well-being that citizens understand the nature of our government and their rights and duties as citizens. The approaching disintegration of political parties and the formation of smaller groups in the nation and in Parliament will further accentuate the need for popular civic instruction. Already the belief which sustained our fathers and grandfathers, that democracy itself was the sovereign remedy for social and political ills, no longer sustains us. The present state of eastern Europe shows that democracy is only safe in the hands of an enlightened people, and that adult suffrage may be the prelude to political decay and national downfall.

Education is the main safeguard of democracy; but the success and stability of democratic government depends very largely on those particular aspects of education which seek to encourage and develop:

(1) the growth of political morality and the community-spirit;

(2) a sound knowledge of the nature of our government and the rights and duties of citizens;

(3) a right understanding of the elements of political economy.

1—2

It is no longer enough that a citizen should know his
duties and rights as a citizen, for, in order to play his
part effectively, he must know the elements of economics,
because industry and commerce are becoming more and
more interwoven with politics. The war has brought this
home to us in the strongest light, and the present exhausted
state of European nations emphasizes the need for mutual
support and international co-operation in economic affairs.
Industrial depression in one country affects other countries;
and at home unemployment and depression in one branch
of industry cause stagnation and depression in another
branch—and so the whole tree is weakened. The unhappy
state of some of our greater industries and the feeling of
helplessness and resentment felt by the masses arise from
ignorance of the simpler laws of economics, which have been
defied, and in consequence the industries and the whole
nation are now suffering.

It is obvious that a knowledge of economics is becoming
essential to citizens of every class, and that such teaching
must be included in any sound scheme of civic instruction
for children or adults. Whether teachers decide to afford
the opportunity for this instruction as part of the teaching
of geography, as suggested in Part III of this book, or
whether they decide to teach the elements of economics as
a separate subject, is not of primary importance. It is the
general recognition of the urgent need for the inclusion
of economic teaching in their schemes of civics which is
important[1].

Teachers who have time and opportunity for those

[1] How *do* "new" subjects become recognized school subjects?
Where does the driving power come from? Does the subject become
a recognized subject because teachers and educationalists think it
worthy and essential—or because outside in the nation there is a
general feeling of the need for such teaching?

branches of social work which enable them to move freely among the working classes and to gain their confidence are struck by the eager demand for enlightenment on economic questions. It is sometimes alleged against adult education that economic and political teaching overburdens the schemes to the detriment of " culture subjects." But people who take this line of argument often forget that in education— and particularly adult education—demand creates supply. On the whole, the schools of a nation are the reflex of the nation and are generally little better or little worse than the nation itself. A nation which is content to muddle along will have an educational system and schools that muddle along. Enlightened citizens may point out the way; but true national education only arises in response to a desire for culture in the majority of citizens. Therefore, can it not be said that the very demand for civic and economic instruction shown in adult schools not only points to a genuine need for such instruction, but is a silent condemnation of the neglect to afford opportunity for such study in schools ?

Further, it must be remembered that youths who leave school often have a voice in deciding matters of national importance in industry, even before they get a vote on political matters. It becomes essential that some well-defined effort should be made in school to teach them the importance of their work, not only as a means of livelihood for themselves, but as a vital factor in the prosperity and welfare of every citizen in the community. However good their intentions and public spirit may be, unless citizens have a reasoned understanding of their obligations to the State and of the elements of economics, they cannot be intelligent citizens. They remain at the mercy of any spurious panacea for social evils.

It is easy for enthusiasts to overstate the part played by national education, and particularly by civic instruction, in general social improvement; and it is courting disappointment to expect too much, for we cannot afford to base our claims for civic instruction in schools *solely* on the ground that it may prove a beneficent social force in the future. "That naïve faith in schooling as a grand panacea for human ills which characterized the age of Bentham and Brougham no longer sustains...nor can we trust implicitly in the diffusion of knowledge, nor even when we accept with Kidd the mighty force of an emotional ideal 'imposed in all its strength through the young' can we trust one generation to settle the destiny of the next."[1] Therefore any scheme of civic instruction worthy of its place in the school curriculum must have other claims. It must have an educational value for school purposes, giving pupils a sound body of useful knowledge and affording them valuable mental training. Otherwise time cannot be found for such teaching in schools, because it is certain that in the present overcrowded state of school curricula some other less valuable subject-matter must give way to make place for civic instruction. The question of how the time is to be found will be treated later. For the present, it is well to ask what attention is being given to civic instruction in the majority of schools to-day. Teachers themselves are the only people who can answer such a question, because the fact that no time is definitely allotted to "civics" or "civic instruction" might convey a wrong impression of the attention given to the subject.

In many schools valuable instruction is being given in this division of culture where no mention of it is made in the timetable; and in others, where time is allotted and "set lessons"

[1] Findlay, *Introduction to Sociology*, Appendix I.

given, very little real instruction is afforded. It must be recognized that many of the "lessons in civics" given in schools to-day are hopelessly dull and educationally value-less[1]. It would be better not to teach the subject at all if it must be dull, for civic instruction which is dull is not only valueless but dangerous. Therefore it is necessary to ensure that the civic instruction in any school complies with a moderate standard of attainment in those aspects of the subject (suitable for school purposes) which are essential to a reasoned understanding of citizenship.

Let us try to define the needs of a young citizen to-day, so that the attention given in school-schemes to these matters may be gauged.

It is not too much to ask that a youth on leaving school shall have received deliberate and systematic instruction in order that he may have:

Firstly—a respect for the institutions of government in the past; and the material and knowledge on which he may be encouraged to build a sound public senti-ment;

Secondly—a knowledge of the machinery and structure of English government to-day, and the duties of a citizen in relation to it;

Thirdly—a knowledge of the elements of economic science, such as the laws of supply and demand, the meaning of wealth, capital, production, exchange, and the im-portance of labour etc.

Lastly, and perhaps most important, his schooling should afford him:

(a) practice in testing the sincerity of human action and

[1] Cf. *British Association Committee on Training in Citizenship* (Section L, Edinburgh, 1921), page 364: "I know one sure way of sickening boys of Civic Duties, and that is to have a lesson called 'Civics.' Any teacher of History who is worth anything of course works it in incidentally." (Opinion from Cheltenham.)

the accuracy of written evidence, so as to give him
training in judgment, observation, and expression[1];

(*b*) some training in self-government, before the struggle
for existence in the world strangles his altruism and
whilst the good of the school is the supreme law.

Although many headmasters may be satisfied with the
provision made in their schools for teaching these subjects,
many more will have the feeling that great improvement
can be made. It must be admitted that in the last few
years much more attention has been given to civics than
formerly. The claims of the subject begin to be pressed by
some teachers, by the Civic Education League, by the
British Association Committee on Training in Citizenship,
and by other bodies. Many books dealing with the subject
have been written and some very helpful school books have
recently been published; but on the whole it is fair to say
that civic teaching is still very much neglected and often
entirely shunned as beyond the purpose of the school or the
function of the teacher.

In schools an ignorance of the elementary facts of citizenship is disclosed from time to time by a chance answer or
question; and teachers who set a simple test-paper, such as
can be found in any good primer of citizenship, will be
surprised at the results, unless their experience is different
from that of the writer. A chance question asked in the
fourth form of a good secondary school first prompted
him to suspect that ignorance of the constitution and its
working to-day which is undoubtedly prevalent in many

---

[1] History and geography can afford scientific training. The material examined is the record of human thought and action. Many
pupils leave schools to-day without ever having had a "printed lie"
pointed out to them; and it is not surprising that they go through
life readily accepting as truth any statement they see in print....
"What can't speak, can't lie!" Thinking, as apart from mere
reading, must be encouraged at all costs.

schools. Only one pupil out of a class of thirty knew the meaning of the letters "J.P." after a man's name. This, of course, is only a trivial thing, but it was significant. Further questions revealed a blissful ignorance of matter which it had been taken for granted the pupils knew. Thus to them the Cabinet meant "Mr. Lloyd George and his friends," and although this might easily be mistaken for precocious political insight, it only showed a care-free, honest ignorance of the English Constitution. It is surprising to find that children in primary schools often have clearer ideas on these matters than older pupils in secondary schools, especially as many of the lessons on civics in some schools, where such lessons are given to-day, are often the dullest and driest of lessons. This is true not only in England but also on the Continent, and it arises not so much from bad teaching as from a false conception of the subject. To limit the scope of civic instruction to a mere catalogue of rights and obligations or a description of the structure of government to-day is to court failure. If the duties of citizenship merely consisted in going to the polling-booth once or twice a year to record a vote, then there would be no need for such teaching. Instruction for livelihood—as apart from instruction for living, for life more abundant—would suffice to enable a young citizen not to spoil a ballot paper. As Professor MacCunn pointed out in his *Ethics of Citizenship* :

That a citizen is enabled to vote, or even that he actually records his vote, this is but a beggarly result of the franchise. The very pith and substance of political citizenship would be gone, were its reality to be measured by the occasions, few and far between, upon which the vote is solicited or recorded....The suggestion is on a par with the doctrine of Rousseau that Englishmen are truly free only when they are engaged in electing members of Parliament.

To-day a citizen needs more than a mere knowledge of our

government and its workings, and some attempt must be
made to encourage civic ideals and the community-spirit.
Whitaker's Almanack, a year-book, a hand-book of civics
no longer suffices as text-books, though they may contain
all the facts that are necessary for a complete grasp of the
form of government, and although much valuable work may
be based on them as books of reference.

Before the value of history and geography was fully recognized, and before the great improvement which has been
effected in the teaching of those subjects in schools had been
made, there was some justification for limiting civic instruction to an outline of our constitution and its working. The
scant attention and the short time given to history and
geography in schools precluded any attention being given
to the rise and development of our constitution or the
economic aspect of geography. Therefore, as the need of
civic instruction was seen in those days, it was thought best
to use a "reader" and base lessons in civics upon it—
treating them as part of a separate subject, with a distinct
subject label[1]. There is no doubt that while the lessons
were sometimes dull, they served a very useful purpose.
They made the best use of the meagre educational facilities
which then existed. But the last decade has seen great
improvement in educational methods, and nowhere has this
been more marked than in the teaching of history and
geography[2]. These two subjects undoubtedly afford the

[1] "While heartily desiring to see history better taught, and to
see it used to illustrate contemporary politics, I look upon civics
as really an easier subject than history, and sufficiently distinct to
deserve an independent place in the curriculum." Viscount Bryce,
1894.
[2] Those who look back and compare the teaching and equipment
afforded in schools to-day with that of fifteen years ago will realize
that there has been almost a new birth of teaching—a veritable
educational Renaissance.

best media for civic instruction, now that serious attention and adequate time are given to them in schools. History, if rightly conceived and presented, can unfold to pupils a panorama of human thought and action, giving not only a useful body of knowledge but also sound mental training. Such teaching ought to give a just appreciation of our common heritage of national ideals, for that is one of the bases on which civic instruction must be founded. Geography must show the toils and labours of "the other fellow" and the economic interdependence of nations, for the understanding of these things is also necessary to intelligent citizenship.

Whatever may have been best and most suitable years ago, it is certain that to divorce civic instruction from history and geography to-day is to impair the value of the instruction and to separate two aspects of history and geography from their rightful position, to the detriment of those subjects themselves. This is especially so in secondary schools where pupils stay for a four-year course; but even in primary schools, the tendency must be to base the teaching of civics more and more on history and geography, which will help to obviate dulness and give the subject coherence and reality.

In *The Living Past* Mr F. S. Marvin has pointed out that it is by looking back that the race gets the courage and often the inspiration to advance. It is equally true of a child climbing up a staircase for the first time, or of a grown man on the field of battle. Looking backwards into history should give us courage, and school history should give pupils a hopeful outlook. It must no longer be a record of battles, plagues, kings, and courtesans, but the record of human progress and endeavour, showing that "all the great sources of human suffering are in a great

degree, many of them entirely, conquerable by human care
and effort." The past must always be brought to bear on
the present, for failure to do this robs history of half its
value. And school history must be so spaced out that the
course finishes with the present time. Much may have to
be abandoned to do this, but it is essential. For instance,
the parallel between the years 1815–22 and 1915–22 is
most instructive and not beyond the grasp of upper forms
in primary or central schools and middle forms in secondary
schools. If the comparison is well worked out, it is laden
with valuable civic teaching, which would be overlooked unless reference is made to the present time and unless careful
study has been given to the nineteenth century.

Similarly with the study of civics. Our Constitution must
be shown as the culmination of a long struggle for liberty
and a long apprenticeship to self-government. It is a noble
heritage, the work of centuries, and bears the impress of
many generations, like the towers of some of our old cathe-
drals. If we neglect to trace the rise and development of
our Constitution, we cannot expect pupils to appreciate its
true value, nor can we hope to stimulate any respect for its
time-honoured institutions. "Other things being equal,"
wrote Bagehot, "yesterday's institutions are the best for
to-day," and if we can lead our pupils to see that English
institutions are the result of centuries of steady, cautious,
English development, then, though they may not realize
it at the time, we are making the institutions of to-day
more intelligible and giving our pupils a worthy ballast
which cannot fail to stabilize their ideas in after-life. The
minutiae of their schooling will be forgotten when they
grow up, so we have to aim at giving them an outlook on
life, a balance and just appreciation of the state and
society, which will abide, rather than a body of knowledge.

Therefore it seems clear that the past holds the key to the present, and that any scheme of civic instruction which has not carefully presented a sketch of civic ideals and government in bygone times must lack vitality; and any short course of lessons dealing with the rights and duties of citizens to-day must not be a separate course, but the completion of work that has progressed throughout the whole school life.

For example: a teacher tells his class that it is the duty of a citizen to assist a policeman in uniform, if he is hard pressed in the execution of his duty; further, that if the policeman calls upon a passer-by for help "in the King's name," the passer-by must render help, and can be punished for failing or refusing to do so. This seems odd to children. They reason to themselves "Why should I risk my head in helping a policeman to arrest a fellow? The policeman is paid to do that sort of thing." But if this duty has been linked up with the past and recalls to a pupil's mind the old English times seven centuries ago, when every man "within the law" was an active guardian of the King's Peace, then what seems a little exacting and unreasonable to-day becomes reasonable and right in their eyes. Although the tythings and the "Hue and Cry" have died out, the King's Peace still remains, and it is still the duty of every citizen to uphold it. Not only are many of the duties of citizenship to-day made more intelligible by being taught through the medium of history or geography, but the teaching of those subjects themselves is improved because a new direction and interest is added. Lessons in citizenship given in their proper setting are much less likely to be dull recitals of rights, duties, and responsibilities, when they stand out clearly against a sound historic background. There is an all-round gain in vitality.

Further, the example set by citizens of the past tends to
encourage and to stimulate public spirit, for it makes a
strong appeal to the community-sense and induces that
respect for public servants and those who have deserved
well of their countrymen which is the surest sign of a
healthy tone in any community, be it a school or a nation.
It may be said that history itself, and especially biography,
will fulfil this aim, without any attempt to re-orientate
the subject with a view to teaching the lessons of citizenship. In a measure this is true, but school history at
present is so largely concerned with the purely political
aspect—kings, rulers, men of war and of action—that
there is a danger of over-working the natural sense of hero-
worship, or, if not of over-working, of misdirecting hero-
worship. There is no doubt that men of valour and prowess
in battle make a more ready appeal to boys than leaders of
thought or of science. This is only to be expected; but if
a civic bias is given to the teaching, and lessons of history
are chosen to show the debt that nations owe to men of
science and to leaders in peace, then this helpful hero-
worship can be directed—" Peace hath her victories...."
Eton will be proud of Lord Roberts, V.C., and East Ham
School will be proud of Jack Cornwell, V.C., as long as boys
are boys; but teachers must correct the balance, for men
like Newton, Kelvin, and Pasteur must not lose their "due
meed of reward."

The war has altered our conception of patriotism, and at
last we see that the true criterion of love of country is
applied social service—giving the best to the community in
time of peace no less than in war. Patriotism used to be
regarded as something a man had or a party had, and
many who boasted it implied that other men and other
parties lacked it. Like all other false conceptions in public

life, this found its reflex in the schools. Teachers often explained and "proved" the greatness of our Empire by pointing to the amount of red on the map—"All that is ours; therefore we are a great people"...and so forth. The greatness of England was vaunted, and to many minds mere repetition brought conviction. After the Boer War there was a general tendency to go to the other extreme and to underrate English ideals and institutions. In some mysterious way it became "good form" to praise things foreign and be contemptuous of things national. This was also reflected in the schools. The history of the British Empire was rejected from many curricula. French and German were given an unduly large share in the time-tables of our secondary schools, while the mother tongue..."Well that'll come of itself, y' know" expressed the attitude.

There are already signs that the war has altered this and clarified our conceptions. We realize now that our citizens —in peace or war—are second to none, and that our educational system, our Constitution and institutions are as good as any in the world. If we want a monument to our greatness, it is around us in the youth and manhood of the Empire, and unless we are to be as ill prepared for the years of peace in the future as we were for the years of war that are past, we must neglect no opportunity for encouraging the community-spirit, for that is the touchstone of citizenship.

Although it is true that public spirit cannot be "taught" or "learnt," schools can do much to foster its growth. Example in this matter is much stronger than precept, but in admitting this we must not overlook the fact that one of the greatest bonds in a school, a regiment, or a nation is the common heritage of ideals.

In the armies of 1915–17 it was found most helpful to

gather the recruits together almost at the outset of their service and to tell them the story of their regiment. The recruits nearly all came away from these "pow-wows" convinced that their regiment was "The" regiment. They felt knit together in no mean way by the story of the deeds and heroism of their bygone comrades, and knew they had something to live up to—a knowledge of the past helped to create "the right spirit" in the present.

To sum up, it seems fair to claim that by teaching (*a*) the political and social aspects of citizenship through the medium of history; and (*b*) the economic aspects of citizenship through the medium of geography:

1. We improve both the teaching of history and geography, giving them added interest and direction;

2. We improve the teaching of civics and save it from becoming abstract and formal;

3. We link up the present with the past, and make history and geography taught in schools lead out into the world of to-day;

4. The most is made of our opportunity to induce respect for time-honoured institutions, and to encourage patriotism and the community-spirit;

5. The teacher of history and geography is assisted in his task of selection;

6. As central and secondary schools are organized at present, adequate civic instruction can be given through these media with the least disarrangement of existing time-tables, and without incurring extra expense or adding a "new" subject to an already over-loaded curriculum.

CHAPTER II

THE CONTENT OF CIVICS FOR SCHOOL PURPOSES

DURING the present century so much has been written about civics and so many phases of civic welfare have been classed as civics, that the subject has become very wide and at the same time rather vague. A glance at the topics to be discussed and the classes and lectures arranged by the Civic Education League at their Summer School shows that the course of civic study embraces almost every aspect of civic welfare[1]. The subjects include among others: the psychology of primitive life, the foundations of civics, public administration, sex education, the causes of infant mortality, the welfare of infants, problems in the use of leisure, town-planning, and the League of Nations. Many of these subjects are quite unsuitable to school work or teaching. In themselves they are stimulating and admirable, but they are essentially studies for the adult mind—indeed they will only interest the relatively few adults who have the desire and aptitude for social service. At the same time the term "Education for Citizenship" has also come to have a very wide scope and application. In a measure all education is now regarded as education for citizenship, because every subject that is taught in school aims directly or indirectly at making the learner a better citizen. Thus

[1] True it is that the Civic Education League were working in co-operation with the National League for Health, Maternity, and Child Welfare and the National Council of Social Service; but all three bodies are doing most valuable work in educating the citizen for the highest ideals of citizenship and might be classed as bodies aiming at the furtherance of civic education.

Milton's description of a complete and generous education might be paraphrased as that which fits a man to perform his duties as a citizen and a man skilfully and magnanimously both in peace and war. In the very breadth of the term "Education for Citizenship" lies the danger that those aspects of education which are definitely directed to teaching a pupil his rights and duties as a citizen and as a member of a community may be disregarded or slurred over. Therefore it seems essential that the content of civics as a school subject must be defined; but at the same time it would be unfortunate if ever the content of civic instruction in schools became so sharply outlined that it left no scope for the individual initiative of teachers, or was not sufficiently elastic to allow for the particular needs of a locality. For instance, a school which is situated in a city or locality with a "storied past" and endowed with interesting historical monuments—say a castle or abbey—would certainly do best to make the most of its local history, even if such a scheme entailed neglect of other important phases. Again, it would be unfortunate if it was ever laid down by the educational authorities exactly what should, and what should not, be taught, as this would restrict the freedom of the teachers and tend to stereotype the teaching. But when all these cautions are weighed and recorded, it is essential that schemes should provide the outlines of a body of knowledge which is indispensable to sound citizenship, and, in order to do this, it is clear that the content of civics for school purposes must be quite definite before beginning the scheme of instruction. Naturally a course of civics suitable for schools would aim at stimulation of future interest in the deeper study of civics as outlined by the Civic Education League; but perhaps the best way to do this is to make sure that the elements of civics are completely grasped, rather than to rely on what must be rather vague and abstract talks on subjects which are beyond the comprehension of most pupils[1].

From time to time opportunities occur in the ordinary course of instruction for valuable incidental teaching of matter which will tend to stimulate interest in many of the wider aspects of civics enumerated above. Thus, although no place can be found in school for any consideration of such a wide subject as town-planning, yet the geography lessons, especially those lessons in descriptive geography which are illustrated by views of well planned towns or cities, *e.g.* Rio, Port Sunlight, modern Paris, are all indirectly lessons in social welfare and in town-planning. The history teacher might spend part of a lesson, when dealing with the years 1666–7, in describing Sir Christopher Wren's plan for rebuilding London and perhaps comparing it with the London which actually grew up when Wren's scheme was rejected. But such teaching must be incidental and indirect. The point to be remembered is that, unless a teacher had kept the civic aspect of history well in mind, such a comparison might have been overlooked, and this and much other valuable incidental teaching would be neglected. These indirect lessons which tend to arouse an abiding curiosity and future interest in civic and social matters rely for their appeal on the power of suggestion.

In arranging a syllabus of instruction, practical teachers are conscious of the limitations and difficulties which hinder almost any new expansion of the school course. These are chiefly restrictions arising from lack of time, the pressure

[1] Thus, during the war, economy was best taught by insisting on the pupils themselves practising those small economies which occur in school life.

of examinations, the competition of the other subjects in the curriculum, the lack of apparatus. But in addition to these difficulties, which arise from considerations of internal administration, any scheme of civic instruction must also conform to the limitations of the average school-boy and the average citizen. True it is that the average school-boy becomes the average citizen in a few years time, but the average school-boy is also a reflex of the average citizen of to-day. Both are characterized by a dislike and distrust of theoretical and abstract knowledge, and they are often similar in their display of indifference towards their respective communities—the school and the state. Therefore in designing a course of civic instruction for the average school-boy, we are at the same time providing for the needs of the average citizen.

In the previous chapter we have already outlined the needs of an average citizen, when setting up a standard by which a headmaster could test the adequacy of the civic instruction given in his school. These were that the pupil's schooling should have afforded him:

I. Some knowledge of the institutions of government in the past, and of the growth of our Constitution;

II. A knowledge of the structure and working of English government to-day and the duties of a citizen in relation to the community, so as to bring out the need for ordered government and institutions, and the obligations of the government, as the trustee of the state, to:

    (1) Defend the community,

    (2) Keep order in the land,

    (3) Judge the people and settle disputes,

    (4) Make laws, to prevent disputes and regulate government; and to make the laws known, so that all citizens may know what is binding on them.

The course must show quite clearly that all citizens are members of the community, having equal civil and political rights and equal obligations; that a citizen is the equal of any other citizen in the courts of justice or the polling-booth; his oath and his vote are as good as any other citizen's, providing he has not discredited his oath and that he uses his vote. In return for the benefits with which the community has endowed him[1], a citizen is bound to uphold the government of the state: he must play his part in defending the country, in helping to maintain order, in helping to render justice to all men, and in voting for representatives who will register the expression of his will in the laws of the land. History must show that all citizens suffer if these institutions of government are not efficiently carried out, and that therefore, even if only from selfish motives, every citizen has a direct interest in helping to carry them out.

The teaching ought to bring these things to the front throughout the whole school course, because these principles are fundamental to citizenship, and must remain when the knowledge of the structure and machinery of government has been forgotten. Also the history course must lead up to a survey of government and public administration as it is to-day, for no pupil should leave school ignorant of the outlines of public administration; and towards the end of school life this survey must be given. It should leave a clear impression of the Crown, its powers and limitations, the chief Ministers of State and their functions; the Law and Justice, the judiciary, from the Lord Chancellor and the Lord Chief Justice to the stipendiary magistrate and the Justice of the Peace; the High Courts and the local courts;

---

[1] Protection, peaceable possession and enjoyment of his property, justice, free schooling for his children, etc., all of which he could not of himself afford.

Parliament, central and local government; taxes, imperial and local (rates); the Poor Laws and their administration; schools and their management; the state regulation of labour; the Army, the Navy, the Police, and how they are governed.

It will be found that this survey, if taken at the end of a course such as is outlined in Part II of this work, will no longer be a dry recital, but one in which the pupils can do most of the work for themselves and which is coherent and educational.

The pupil should also have acquired:

III. A knowledge of the elements of economic science—the laws of supply and demand, the meaning of wealth, capital, production, distribution, exchange and the function of labour in the creation of wealth etc.;

IV. Some training in self-government, and definite training to enable the pupil to use his judgment and to distinguish truth from untruth in written evidence.

Are there any other lessons that can be taught in school which are valuable from the point of definite training for citizenship? If so, every opportunity must be taken to see that they are included in the content and scope of our teaching. They may be set down in order of importance thus:

1. THE IMPORTANCE OF HONEST WORK.

History and geography as taught in schools should bring out quite clearly that the brain and muscle of the members of any community are its greatest assets and its true wealth producers; and that, whether a man earns his livelihood by "brain work" or by manual labour (also largely brain work), he cannot be a good or useful citizen unless he does fair and good work.

2. THE IMPORTANCE OF THE RIGHT USE OF LEISURE.

Modern technical inventions and improvements have increased production a thousandfold and enable man to enjoy a higher standard of comfort (not necessarily of civilization or culture) than ever before. The greatest benefit might well be regarded as the great increase of leisure. In dealing with modern social legislation, such as the eight-hour day etc., it can be pointed out that the happiness and welfare of the community depend very largely on the use or abuse of leisure. In this respect much good work is being done by the "hobby clubs" which are so popular in many schools, for it is in such ways that boys learn the true meaning of recreation[1].

3. THE IMPORTANCE OF HYGIENE AND NATIONAL HEALTH.

Most courses of civics designed for reading in primary schools emphasize the need for a study of the problem of health—ventilation, sanitation, suitable food, personal cleanliness, etc. In some primary schools this phase of civics is very necessary; but at the same time the amount that can be learnt is so small that probably the best way to teach these lessons in schools is—always, of course, apart from insisting on personal cleanliness and ventilation etc.—by encouraging games, gymnastics, swimming, and other forms of exercise[2]. The gymnastic instructor of to-day has replaced the drill sergeant, and he demonstrates the value of health in the most direct and attractive manner. In secondary schools the need of definite instruction or direction in these

[1] It is strange that in English schools—for we are the most sportsmanlike and games-loving people in the world—so few history textbooks or syllabuses ever give any attention to the history and rise of our national sports.

[2] And for girls an expansion and improvement in the teaching of domestic science, care of children, etc.

matters is perhaps less than in the primary schools, and therefore, beyond the incidental teaching, it is not proposed to include health lessons in the scope of civics outlined in this chapter—though it is undoubtedly an important phase of civics in its larger aspect.

4. THE IMPORTANCE OF EDUCATION.

It used to be said that one half of the world did not know how the other half lived. Certainly to-day one half of the English people does not know how the other half is educated; and it is scarcely remarkable that popular education is often regarded with suspicion as an expensive outcrop of modern civilization by many otherwise enlightened people.

Is it too much to ask that pupils in primary and secondary schools should know something of the rise of modern national education and of the rise of a national system in England? Surely in a four-year course of history some time could be found for an outline of this subject. In most of the newer readers and books of elementary civics written for school use some outline of the progress of popular education is given, and there are other signs that attention is accorded to this, which is perhaps the most striking and far-reaching development of the last fifty years.

These, then, are the chief aspects of civic instruction desirable and suitable to teach in schools. The subjects outline the scope of civics as a school subject without unduly restricting it. Although the whole forms a coherent and useful body of knowledge, yet, without undue compression and restriction, it cannot be formulated like arithmetic into a synthesis of rules, for this would tend to make civics a formal and dry-as-dust subject and be fatal to successful teaching.

It is not altogether desirable to have a text-book or primer of civics in schools, except as an outline on which to base the work of the last few terms or as a summary. Up to the present it has been convenient in primary schools to use such books, and of late some excellent readers and primers have been published for primary and continuation schools. But, with the improvement in the teaching of history and geography in schools, it will be found that civic instruction can be more adequately and suitably presented through the media of those subjects themselves. It is for this reason that better civic teaching is often given in schools where there is no text-book or reader of civics, and no mention of civics or citizenship in the time-table, than in schools which devote a period a week to civics. Naturally such a wide subject cannot possibly be dealt with by one teacher only. Just as all English teachers are teachers of English, so all teachers ought to regard themselves as teachers of civics. The history, geography, English, and science masters, and those in charge of gymnastic and domestic instruction, must all help and play their part. The history and geography specialists will take the largest share of the instruction, because their subjects afford more opportunity and scope for civic instruction, but the best results can only be obtained if every member of the staff seeks out and makes the most of every opportunity which his subject offers to impart civic instruction. Thus, for instance, a science master who fails to give his pupils some account of the life and work of the greater scientists whose work may be under study in his lecture-theatre or laboratory, is not making the most of his subject or of his opportunities for imparting knowledge which is of definite value as a preparation for citizenship[1]. Some

[1] At West Square Central School, Southwark, the science master has made cards which are admirably illustrated and designed. Each

knowledge of Boyle, Newton, Ohm, Kelvin as men, rather than mere names, must make the subject more interesting, quite apart from any value such knowledge may have in helping a pupil to form a habit of mind which disposes him to judge men's worth in terms of their services to mankind. At present, few history teachers have enlarged the scope of their subject so as to include some outline of the growth of scientific thought ; while few science teachers feel it part of their duty to enlighten their pupils as to the lives and personalities of the scientists—and thus valuable teaching falls between two stools. It is the more regrettable because it could so easily be avoided by collaboration, and because both the teaching of history and natural science would benefit by being brought into closer touch with life.

one shows a picture of a famous scientist, his nationality, birthplace, dates and period, his school and work-place, and the discoveries and work for which he is famous. When the work of any of these men of science is under study, or if it is the anniversary or centenary of any particular scientist, then his picture and record are exhibited in the calendar or roll of honour and a short talk is held about him and his work. The pupils themselves often volunteer to execute these cards in their spare time, and the frame and cards form perhaps the most treasured and certainly not the least valuable exhibit in the laboratory.

CHAPTER III

DIFFICULTIES OF WEAVING IN THE SUBJECT

ASSUMING that responsible teachers accept the content of the subject outlined above as adequate and practicable, and realize that civic instruction must be given in schools because it is an aspect of humanism which has been neglected in the past, but which social and political conditions demand shall be no longer neglected or left to chance, they are then faced with the difficulty of weaving in the subject. Firstly, there is the fear of laying themselves open to the charge of special pleading, or of "putting ideas into the children's heads." Secondly, there is the lack of time, which is aggravated by the pressure of examinations and the overcrowded state of the curriculum. And thirdly, there is the difficulty of collecting suitable material—illustrative matter, on which pupils may be set to work to find out for themselves truths which would otherwise merely have to be expounded by the teacher, and so lose in value and directness and probably make little appeal to the pupils, because the search for truth is often of greater educational value than the truth itself.

It is obvious that some matter which is taught at present must be abandoned and a rigid selection made, to find time for many new aspects which have been outlined in the syllabus of civics. The work will have to be graded and spread over the whole school period.

Let us suppose a headmaster feels that much more attention could be given to civic instruction in his school than is being given at present, and that he calls a meeting of his colleagues responsible for the teaching of history, geography, and English to discuss the question. In the matter of civic instruction such conferences are vital, because unity of aim and of outlook among the various teachers is essential to the well-being of the scheme. As these and other specialists are going to collaborate, it is necessary that they should know which aspects each of them is going to teach, in order to prevent overlapping and waste of time. Further, as it is impossible to give civic or political instruction without constant reference to modern social and political conditions, it is important that these colleagues should have similar aims. It is not, however, necessary or even desirable that they should agree in their political outlook, because they are not propagandists, and are not going to teach what they think to be true or desirable, but rather to lead the pupils to think for themselves and to see the result of others' thought, or want of thought, in the past and in the present. At times it may be difficult to forget political bias, but by scrupulous fairness this can be overcome and balance maintained. It is the search for truth and the habit of searching which must be encouraged; and therefore this meeting and collaboration is an excellent starting-point for any sound scheme of civic instruction, because, apart from any stimulus given to the subject, the teachers responsible for the humanist studies "agree to agree" in their aims and, as far as possible, in their methods.

In view of the large measure of freedom allowed to senior masters in charge of subjects and the invariable care and skill with which in modern secondary schools they work out their schemes and syllabuses, it may seem that the part played by the "Head" is being over-emphasized; but if the headmaster regards himself as chairman of the board of civic instruction in the school, then his staff know that they have his support, and the teaching gains in a measure only known to those who are intimate with school life. Games, music, or art are often said to be "features of the school," and usually this can be traced to the influence, if not the actual teaching, of the headmaster. His wishes and predilections, sometimes his foibles and idiosyncracies, filter down to the most junior scholar, for the desire to please the Head is a potent and very human motive in scholars and teachers alike. Why should it not be said that civics is a feature of the school? Or better, why should not civic instruction be a feature of all schools, so that it goes without saying that the school's first pride is in turning out young people with a clear idea of their duties as citizens and a capacity and desire for social service?

Once this is definitely established as an aim of the school, opportunities will be found in plenty for valuable teaching from the point of preparation for citizenship. The history master decides to be responsible for the greater part of the political aspect of civic instruction, the geography master for the chief share of the economic, and preferably some other master is asked to begin a scheme of class self-government—then the scheme may be said to have started. But the first, though not the greatest, difficulty is the lack of time. Both the history and geography teachers would wish for "another period a week" to be allocated to their subjects, and headmasters, with the best intentions in the world, must find this so difficult, in the present state of the curriculum, as to be impossible. Therefore the masters are thrown back on a rigid selection and testing of the subject-matter which they have grown to regard as essential, and which the syllabuses of external examinations seem to make essential. It is obvious that time cannot be found for any adequate consideration of the rights and duties of citizens in the past and present, a study (even an outline) of our constitutional history, and the particular study of the last century, unless there is a very careful pruning.

THE QUESTION OF EXAMINATIONS

A point which will occur to practical teachers is how the syllabus can be reconciled with the demands of external examinations. Lessons devoted to the civic aspects of history and geography are not likely to be well spent if "satisfying the examiners" is the sole end of the teaching, because it is unlikely that, for some time at any rate, the pupils will be examined upon that aspect of their training or instruction. This is to be regretted in so far as it is an admission of the lack of standing that civic instruction has in the eyes of those who control and direct the more important public examinations; but it has the advantage that the absence of examination gives the teacher greater scope and freedom in teaching. Probably the advantages outweigh the disadvantages. Unfortunately it is true that, to a considerable extent, subjects in which pupils are not examined are very often not taught; and the particular danger to civic instruction of any kind is that, as the standard of examination in history and geography tends to become higher each year, so any time which might be devoted to this aspect will be so restricted as to nullify or even to cut out the teaching altogether. Teachers must face this difficulty, and if they have decided to devote a small portion of the time allotted to history and geography to the study of material helpful in the formation of civic ideals, then they must firmly resist that pressure which will "crowd out" those lessons, and reserve the allotted periods for the study of the selected material.

It is very difficult to do this in practice and yet not to give too much time to the phases of historical or geographical teaching which were chosen for their value as indirect civic instruction, because *all* history teaching is humanizing and valuable. Each teacher must decide for himself what is reasonable in his special circumstances, but, having decided, it is to be hoped that examinations will not cause him to turn down his original scheme. If, owing to the nearness of an examination, a teacher is tempted to do so, especially when his pupils reach the critical age of fifteen to sixteen years, some comfort may be found in the reflection that the more popular school examinations in history and geography tend more and more to test and reward intelligence and judgment, rather than merely to demand a ready knowledge of facts, dates, or place-names. If these special lessons are taught in the right spirit, they afford considerable scope for training judgment and for intelligent appreciation of historical values; and the pupil who may be hazy about the battles of the Wars of the Roses, or the sieges and affrays of the Civil War, will probably gain a higher place than another pupil whose instruction has been specially moulded to suit the syllabus of the examination. The right kind of examination forms a valuable educational process and is a real test of merit, but the "right kind" never fetters the teaching; and as for the wrong kind, headmasters can easily alter them by not allowing their scholars to sit for them.

The Accusation of Special Pleading

The danger of being accused of special pleading, of putting ideas into the children's heads, has been greatly exaggerated. School history cannot afford to be colourless, and vigorous teaching must often leave decided and vigorous impressions; but providing the teacher gets balance in his subject matter, he is unlikely to leave a biassed or jaundiced impression on the minds of the pupils. It must be remembered that so many bodies have urged propaganda in schools that democracy is suspicious—and rightly so—of any form of special pleading for or against any of the "isms" which afflict us to-day. The attitude of the teacher must be one of absolute impartiality and sterling sincerity. He is wisest who regards himself as the leader of a class searching for truth, rather than a giver of truth. " Do not imagine you are listening to me. It is history itself that speaks " is as true for the teacher of history in the school as for the professor in the university. The teacher of history must not only aim at impartiality in the presentation, but equally in the selection, of his subject-matter. For instance, if, in dealing with the Reformation in the reign of Edward VI, the teacher has brought out the unenviable greed of Somerset and Northumberland and their followers in the ignoble race for Church spoils, it is only fair to balance the impression with some account, say, of the Oxford martyrs who re-established the cause of the Reformation in the eyes of decent Englishmen. This balance and impartiality in selection is most important, especially in dealing with recent history. In teaching the social life of the nineteenth century it is fatally easy to present a picture of the misery of working-people, which leaves a false impression more from its narrowness and the exclusion of the other side of the picture than from any bias in presentation[1]; and as the intelligent study of the nineteenth century forms the broadest channel for civic instruction offered by the school course, particular care must be taken to be free from this form of partiality or one-sidedness[2].

[1] Cf. Gilbert Slater, *The Making of England.*
[2] A study of the accounts of the War of Independence as written in the history text-books used in American schools will show how

The Collection of Illustrative Material

The difficulty experienced by the teacher in the collection of documents of local and national importance on which exercises can be based, and which can be used for illustrative purposes, is rather one of lack of time than lack of material. The work of Messrs Keatinge and Frazer and others has given teachers and pupils access to good collections of documents of national importance. But for busy specialists in many schools it is difficult to find time to seek out documents of local importance. The Victoria County Histories are a great help in this matter, and the local antiquary can usually be most helpful. Thus in Clitheroe (Lancs.) much useful material was found in the records of the Courts—the Halmotes, Courts Leet and Baron, etc.—on which the writer was able to build lessons showing the working of old-time justice and the maintenance of order and local government. A teacher going into a new district will invariably find that the local librarian, even if he himself is not interested, knows the people in the district who are keenly interested in local lore and who would be willing to help. Naturally it takes some time to make their acquaintance, but it is fortunate that districts which have a "storied" past, and in which local history is most helpful to the teacher, usually are not lacking in antiquarian lore, and so the teacher's task is lightened.

far such partiality may go; and a knowledge of the less cultured American people will show the harm this has done to Anglo-American relations.

THE SYLLABUS

The following history syllabus is fairly representative of the modern secondary school; and it is necessary to examine the content of the syllabus closely to decide how much time must be set aside for a course, extending throughout the whole school life, dealing with the rights and duties of citizens and the growth of the Constitution, and also to decide what aspects or phases of history will have to give place in order that time may be found for the new work.

1ST YEAR.

1st term. Outlines of Greek history.

2nd term. Outlines of Roman history.

3rd term. Reading from European history from break-up of the Roman Empire down to the time of Peter the Great (largely biographical).

2ND YEAR.

1st term. Outline of English history from the beginning to 1066.

2nd term. English history, 1066–1485 (with special reference to Henry II and Edward I).

3rd term. Life in Middle Ages (Social and Constitutional).

3RD YEAR.

1st term. Outline of English history, 1485–1603.

2nd term. Outline continued to 1714.

3rd term. Constitutional and social review of the period.

4TH YEAR.

1st term. English history, 1714–1815.

2nd term. The making of modern England, 1815 to present day.

3rd term. Constitutional and social review of the nineteenth century, and study of special topics.

5TH YEAR.

1st term. Outline of European history from 1815 onwards.

2nd term. Sketch of American history in outline, especially the Civil War and Abraham Lincoln. Outline of American Government and Constitution.

3rd term. Outline of the growth of the British Empire, with special reference to modern political conditions and government to-day.

A study of: *The Principles of Citizenship* (Sir H. Jones); *The Ethics of Citizenship* (John MacCunn).

The Question of Time

If the time allotted to history in school is two periods a week, supplemented by two periods of preparation or homework, that would mean 104 school periods a year, less 24 for vacations, which leaves about 80 periods. Now in a school where the text-book is of the old type, fairly full and largely political in character, a teacher will need to devote more time to the special lessons he designs as "civic" in their aim than would be necessary in a school using text-books which have a constitutional and social bias[1]. The best teachers of history and geography are becoming more and more independent of the text-books, and are relying to a much greater extent on documents and illustrative matter which they collect and arrange for themselves. Indeed, the expensive history text-book is happily giving place to shorter and more concise sketches supplemented and illustrated by documents which form the basis of instruction, under the teacher's direction. There is no comparison between the quality of work done by a class using such a book and one using the older and more substantial text-book, for the former gives more scope both to the pupils and the teacher. Therefore it seems certain that if the text-book is to remain, as in a measure it must, the basis of the teaching, shorter sketches and outlines of history must be used. In this way it is possible to cover in outline the period for the year's study in the first two terms, leaving the third term free for closer study of the social and civic aspects of the period. Not only is time saved by treating the subject in this way, but the work gains in coherence and continuity. It is possible to give special attention to a particular reign or a particular aspect of the period for

[1] *E.g.* Keatinge and Frazer, *History of England for Schools.*

which no time can be found if the outline is too full. The reason why so many aspects of history are crowded out is very largely because the whole time is taken in " covering the ground," leaving no time for the study of documents or particular phases of development. Many careful and conscientious teachers of history do not get the best results because of this; their treatment is too strictly chronological, too full, and too even. Nothing stands out; their presentation of the subject is more like a film picture at the cinema than a good dramatic presentation at the theatre. Evenness of treatment does not impress pupils. The great battle-scene painted around the walls of the colonnade of the courtyard at Les Invalides fails to impress an adult, for, on looking back, no single episode or group stands out in one's mind. If the teacher decides that in the first term, consisting of approximately twenty-two lessons, six must be given to the consideration of the life of the Athenian citizen, his rights and duties, then he knows that the outline must be curtailed so as to leave three weeks for this phase of his subject. But it is not possible to indicate the point at which these lessons can be given most advantageously, nor to lay down that they are best given in sequence. These are matters which experience will decide. As a rule they are more effective when given as a course of lessons in sequence, and usually somewhere towards the end of term is the better time, because the class has then had an outline of the period which forms a background for the lessons. But in the case of the third term's work in the first year, where there is so much ground to be covered, no time could be given, and also none is called for, owing to the nature of the survey, because the work is simply reading for information and interest. The lessons on Greek and Roman citizenship fall into their places towards the end of the terms in which the Greek and Roman periods are under study.

Again, in the second year (first term), when the history of England to the Conquest is set, the end of term would be the most suitable time for the course of lessons designed to form an introduction to the consideration of the rights and duties of English citizenship. Thus :

Lesson 1. Communities and their Government.

Lesson 2. Illustrations from Caesar and Tacitus showing the Government of our early ancestors.

Lesson 3. Outline of Anglo-Saxon Government.

Lesson 4. Outline of Anglo-Saxon Government (continued).

Lesson 5. Revision lesson emphasizing, among other topics:

    (*a*) No rights without duties in Anglo-Saxon times, *e.g.* King, Earls, Thegns, Freemen, Serfs.

    (*b*) The growing tendency to make possession of land the badge (criterion) of freedom.

    (*c*) The great importance of local government as the early training ground in self-government, and the strength of the local community-spirit.

    (*d*) The geographical and economic difficulties which prevented the ordinary freeman taking part in the government of the shire, save by representatives, or spokesmen.

    (*e*) The factors at work which tended to consolidate the Anglo-Saxon peoples into the English, and the difficulties (racial, geographic, economic) which tended to modify and hinder the development of central government.

These lessons form an introduction to the study of the English Constitution and to the future understanding of the limitations and greatness of the English peoples; they aim also at laying the foundation of the political and civic education of the pupils.

By frequent comparison with what pupils learnt of Greece and Rome (in the first year's work) differences and likenesses can be emphasized. Thus, for instance, the tendency to make the possession of land the badge of the freeman may be compared with the Athenian social classes based on land ownership. Again, the idea of the wealthier freemen equipping themselves as horse-soldiers (or taking up the duties of thegnship) can be compared with Athenian military duties. Such factors as communal responsibility and its expression in Anglo-Saxon law and custom ("no landless man shall be without a lord"), the difficulties of policing districts, the importance in early justice of the good-will and testimony of neighbours, all lead pupils to appreciate tendencies which, developed at a later date, influenced the growth of our national system of government.

Lessons with similar aims can be given throughout the four-year course leading up to a final revision of the system and nature of government to-day, which in turn leads to a wider and deeper survey of an international nature in the fifth year, if time can be found for such a course in view of the pressure of examinations. In this way throughout the whole school course, without more time being given to the study of history, definite and deliberate attention can be given to those aspects of history which prepare the pupil for intelligent citizenship. In learning to know the English people they learn to know themselves, for pupils are encouraged to look back into history, to look around to-day, and to look into the future; they gain balance, and see that, though conditions have altered, the English people are animated to-day by much the same motives as they were in the past. This knowledge of the race is the surest and safest foundation for the civic instruction of the English people.

PART II

A SCHEME OF CIVIC INSTRUCTION BASED ON HISTORY SHOWING THE FUNCTION OF HISTORY IN THE TEACHING OF CIVICS

A TYPICAL HISTORY SYLLABUS

Year	Term	History
First (Form I)	Autumn	Outlines of Ancient History, especially Greek History (Book I, *The Story of the World*)
	Spring	Outlines of Roman History and Dark Ages Outline of History of Middle Ages (Book II, *The Story of the World*)
	Summer	The Middle Ages (continued) and The Age of Discovery (Book III, *The Awakening of Europe*)
Second (Form II)	Autumn	English History from beginning to about 1066 A.D.
	Spring	English History from 1066 A.D. to about 1485 A.D.
	Summer	Social History—Life in the Middle Ages
Third (Form III)	Autumn	English History, 1485 A.D. to about 1603 A.D.
	Spring	English History from 1603 A.D. to 1714 A.D.
	Summer	Social History, 1485 A.D. to 1714 A.D.
Fourth	Autumn	English History in outline from 1714 A.D. to about 1815 A.D.
	Spring	The History of England in the Nineteenth Century (1815 to the Armistice)
	Summer	Social Life in the Nineteenth Century Studies of particular topics (see pp. 118 foll.)
Fifth	...	For suggested courses see page 34

COURSE BASED ON THE FOREGOING SYLLABUS

FIRST YEAR

1. AUTUMN TERM. Stories from Ancient History—especially of Hellas.
2. SPRING TERM. Stories from Roman History—The Dark Ages and the Middle Ages.
3. SUMMER TERM. Continuation of Stories—The Middle Ages — The Age of Discovery — The Dawn of Modern History, etc.

AUTUMN (1ST) TERM

Syllabus. The chief stories of Hebrew, Phoenician, and Greek history, dealing with Abraham—Joseph—Hiram of Tyre —,Solomon — Carthage — The Siege of Troy— The Founding of Rome—The Dawn of History—The Fall of Tyre—The Rise of Carthage—The East—Persians—The Clash of East and West—The Battle of Marathon—Leonidas—Athens—Sparta—Salamis—The Beauty of Athens —Pericles—Socrates—The War with Sparta—Macedon— Alexander the Great—Egypt—Syria—The Greek Colonies —The Rise of Roman Power.

Time. About twenty-five periods may be allowed for history in the term, supplemented by twenty-five periods of homework or preparation. Of this number, six school periods and an equal number of preparation may be devoted to special lessons which aim at giving pupils an account of the civic life of Athens and the intense civic pride and patriotism of the Athenians. The most suitable point in the syllabus at which to give these lessons is best decided by the teacher, but it is advisable to give them in sequence, preferably towards the end of the term after the class has read down to the death of Socrates.

LESSONS SUGGESTED TO ILLUSTRATE
ATHENIAN CITIZENSHIP

1. *The City State of Athens.*
2. *The People of Athens*—Slaves, Aliens, Citizens.
3 & 4. *The Citizens*—their rights and duties.
5. *Pericles*, the first great public servant, and his famous oration.
6. *The Fathers of Citizenship*, Plato and Aristotle.
    Conclusion—Our debt to Hellas.

LESSON 1. THE CITY STATE OF ATHENS.

The class will be familiar with the map of ancient Greece, and particularly with Attica and the Bay of Salamis, from their reading and work in term. On a large scale plan of Athens, of which pupils have smaller copies, the chief buildings may be marked, particularly the Parthenon, the Erechtheum, the Statue of Athena the Champion, the theatre of Dionysus, and the white-stepped Propylaea leading to the fortress city.

It is helpful to compare the distance from the Piraeus with some well-known local distance. An aeroplane photo of Athens to-day is most useful, and can be followed by pictures of the chief ruins and afterwards of the buildings as restored, and also by drawings and plaster casts of statues etc. This all gives colour and arouses curiosity as to the sort of people who built and lived in Athens. It must be pointed out that the houses of the poorer citizens were often poor and simple, but rarely squalid and mean. Also that the Athenians lived out of doors a great deal and that they felt that the city was their home in a more intimate way than is possible for people living the cold indoor-life of northern cities. They enjoyed and used their public buildings (gymnasia, theatres, and temples) far more than we do.

Again, the size of Attica will need emphasis; and comparison, say with Yorkshire, is useful. But it must be pointed out that this was a State, a City State, proud and independent. The fact that a farmer on the slope of Pentelicus was a citizen of Athens seems strange to pupils who have to get rid of the idea which associates an Athenian with a Londoner and have rather to think of a "Britisher" in order to get a true comparison. But when they see that this farmer used to get up early and trudge into Athens to vote in the Assembly or to sit on a jury, then they realize that it was not merely residence, but membership of a community, which made him an Athenian citizen, just as surely as if he lived under the shadow of the Acropolis itself. The city was the State, and the farmer felt his farm to be a part of the city, of the "polis." The size of the State can be brought home to pupils by asking them to imagine a man in the upper seats of the theatre of Dionysus on a clear day and to picture how far he could see—practically half the State; while if Athena the Champion had come to life on her high pedestal, she could have overlooked the whole State. It might be suggested that the Athenian preference for small States was due to the fact that they could not conceive any State so large that a citizen living in the most remote parts could not regularly take a personal share in the government; and if a State was so large that citizens like our farmer could not get to the Assembly, do his duty by recording his vote, and get home again the same night, then they felt that such a State would be dangerously overgrown and politically unhealthy.

NOTES TO LESSON 1

1. Perhaps it was considered rather risky to live in places from which one could not see the sunrise or sunset gilding the spear of Athena's statue.

2. This lesson can be rounded off by reading a description of Athens in her prime, such as may be found in the opening pages of H. de Vere Stacpoole's book, *The Street of the Flute Player*.
3. For useful illustrations, plans, and notes, see Keatinge and Frazer, *An Introduction to World History*, chap. iv. For the most helpful account of Athenian life and government, see A. E. Zimmern, *The Greek Commonwealth*; also the brief review of Greek life and thought in chap. xxii of H. G. Wells' *Outline of History* is helpful.

LESSON 2. THE PEOPLE OF ATHENS.

The first lesson ought to have stimulated a healthy curiosity as to the sort of people who lived in Athens, and the present lesson will therefore aim at giving the class an understanding of how the Athenians lived and more particularly how they governed themselves. In directing attention to the civic life of Athens care must be taken to give enough colour to the scheme to redeem the lesson from mere abstractions; but pupils can easily see that in any community the people may be classified or grouped in many different ways, such as by birth, family, or tribe, by their work, or according to their wealth (either in flocks, in land, or in money), or lastly by the part they play in the civic life of the State. Furthermore there is a certain rough sequence in such classification, beginning with birth or family in the small clan or tribal community, and leading onwards to the part a man plays in the State—his civic standing—in the larger and more highly civilized community, such as a City State.

From the work of the term pupils will have realized that in every community from the smallest group, the family, to the largest, the nation, there must be people (i) who work, (ii) who are prepared and able to defend the community, (iii) who keep order, and (iv) who rule and are responsible[1].

[1] Perhaps it is not too early to point out that the share taken by the people in (ii), (iii), and (iv) determines the type of government—despotism, democracy, etc.

These are the universal features of ordered and peaceable community life and essentials to peace and progress. The outline of Greek history will already have shown pupils that the Athenians set more store on what a man did for the State than on what he did for himself and his own family, and that they valued public spirit very highly and expected every man who had civic rights to perform his civic duties promptly and with diligence.

Therefore the natural sequence of the lessons seems to be a study of: (i) the slaves in Athens, (ii) the aliens in Athens, and (iii) the Athenians (citizens).

(i) *The Slaves in Athens.*

In dealing with slavery it is important to point out that slavery was regarded as part of the natural order of things, and also to describe the humane way in which slaves were treated by the Athenians (as compared with Sparta, for instance); but it is essential to describe the work they did in Athens, the part they played in the economic life of the city, and to emphasize the fact that it was the presence of such numbers of slaves and the work they performed that made it possible for the Athenians to have leisure, and enabled them to give a larger portion of their time to civic affairs than would be possible for the majority of people in non-slave-owning States of modern times. This drives home the economic aspect of citizenship, on which all civil and political progress depends, but which is only too easily overlooked.

(ii) *The Alien dwellers in Athens.*

The tolerant, even benevolent, attitude of the Athenian citizens towards aliens cannot be grasped unless the work they did, their services to trade, to finance, and to shipping, is described, and unless it is pointed out that in the age of

Pericles there was practically no such thing as unemployment in Athens. Further, the Athenians, though often
keen farmers and splendid artisans and craftsmen, rather
"looked down their noses" at trade. It will be seen that
the aliens had civil rights—they were protected by the laws;
but they had no political rights, that is, no direct voice in
the making of laws or the administration of justice; though,
of course, like all resident aliens, especially Jews, by their
wealth and industry they were often able to influence, and
sometimes sensibly affect, state policy.

LESSONS 3 AND 4. THE CITIZENS OF ATHENS.

The most helpful introduction to this lesson on the rights
and duties of Athenian citizens will probably be a brief
revision of the work of Solon, paying attention to the work
attributed to him in:

(i) Grouping citizens on a basis of land-holding and allocating
duties and obligations correspondingly graded — *e.g.* richer
classes serving in the army as cavalry whilst poorer citizens
served as lightly armed foot-soldiers.

(ii) Making the assembled people the supreme court of appeal and
giving them power to call upon the magistrates to account for
their acts during their terms of office.

(iii) Giving the Athenians a written code of laws.

Some reference will also be necessary to the reforms of
Cleisthenes in making the government more democratic, and
particularly to his regrouping all citizens into demes or
"people-groups," which became the units of local government and the little civic communities from which people
went up in turn to play their part in the central government of the City State. This will lead up to a review of
the chief features of Athenian government—the demes,
the Council (central administrative body); the jurors and
the system of large juries, the outstanding feature of the

judicial system; and lastly the Assembly, the meeting of the sovereign people—the supreme judicial and legislative gathering.

An outline such as this will fully occupy the whole period, but it can be made much more interesting than a formal presentation of the rights and duties of citizens. It is a necessary preliminary to a reasonable grasp of civic rights and duties; and if pupils have been warned at the outset of the lesson to be on the look-out for the rights and duties of the citizens, and have had an opportunity to jot down notes during the course of the lesson, it gives interest to the lesson and coherence to the outline.

The tabulation of the duties under the four headings— (i) Defence, (ii) Order, (iii) Justice, and (iv) Law-making— forms a suitable task for preparation and ensures independent work. Part of the next period may then be devoted to correcting and amplifying their efforts, as below:

At the time of Pericles the chief duties of an Athenian citizen would be to:

1. *Help to defend the State.* Not merely to be willing, but *prepared*, to serve in the army or navy, equipped according to his rank and wealth. Although military service was compulsory, it was a privilege and a citizen's first duty.

2. *Help to keep order.* As there were no police except the small guards on the harbour, treasury, and the citadel, all helped to suppress disorder or wrong-doing; *e.g.* Solon's ideal "The city in which all citizens, whether they have suffered injury or not, equally pursue and punish injustice."

3. *Help to administer justice.* The Athenians loved fair play and also thought that there was "safety in numbers"; therefore their juries were large, rarely less than two hundred, and the whole people gathered together in the Assembly formed the supreme court of appeal. As many as 6000 citizens would be engaged as jurors on days when there were many suits to be heard.

4. *Help to make laws* in the Assembly. Although new laws were rarely made, and "The Law" or "The Laws" usually meant Solon's code, yet the Athenians firmly believed and acted upon the saying "what touches all must be discussed by all."

In discussing and tabulating the above it will be necessary to emphasize points like the following:

The numbers of citizens in proportion to the total who might be (and often actually were) engaged on affairs of State. It was open to any citizen to be president of his deme, and consequently president of the Council, for one day; which meant that for the time he would be the acting head of the State, keeping the keys of the treasury and of the citadel, guarding the public records and the great seal of the State. The Athenians had no bureaucracy; they scorned to rule or be ruled by deputies; for they loved speaking for themselves and so had little use for spokesmen; they counted a man who took no part in civic affairs " not as harmless but as useless." It was a restless, surging, civic life, and though the people made many mistakes and the mob was often fickle and treacherous, they had a zeal for service and an undying love for their country which, under the guidance of men like Pericles, made them the greatest nation of antiquity.

LESSON 5. PERICLES.

From their reading earlier in the term pupils will be familiar with the character of Pericles, and it will only be necessary to emphasize his work as the first great public servant. A period may be spent in reading extracts from the funeral oration simplified and loosely adapted from Thucydides as below; and as home-work pupils can be asked to write down what they learn about the duties of citizens from the speech :

B.C. 431.—These were the first that had fallen, and Pericles, son of Xanthippus...advanced from the sepulchre to a raised platform... and spoke as follows:
(Here follows an introduction to the main speech, dealing with the law which made a funeral oration over dead heroes a public duty, and in praise of the ancestors of the State.)

"Our Constitution does not copy the laws of surrounding States—we are rather a pattern to others than imitators...government is in the hands of the many instead of the few; this is why it is called a democracy....The laws afford equal justice to all...advancement in public life falls to reputation for ability and worth...for a man's class does not interfere with merit...nor does poverty bar the way to advancement in public life...if a man is able to serve the State he is not hindered because he is not well known. We are easy in our private relations with one another...but this does not make us lawless citizens.

"Further we provide plenty of means for recreation...we celebrate games and sacrifices all the year round, and the elegance of our private houses forms a daily source of pleasure, driving away dull care....The greatness of our city attracts the commerce of the world to our harbours....

"In military policy too, we differ from our enemies, trusting to the inborn spirit of our citizens. In education...we are not harsh. At Athens we live freely, yet are prepared for every danger....

"We are lovers of the beautiful, simple in our tastes; we cultivate virtue without loss of manliness.

"Wealth we employ more for use than ostentation, and count the real disgrace of poverty not in admitting it, but in refusing to struggle against it....We regard a man who takes no interest in the affairs of State not as harmless but as useless....We Athenians can decide what is best even if we cannot originate...and we carefully discuss every action of State before carrying it out....We are generous, and make friends and allies by granting, rather than receiving, favours....In short, I say, Athens is the School of Hellas...and I doubt if any other State can produce citizens who are so well fitted to meet any emergency and who are so many-sided in their interests. Such is Athens...and it is for such a city these heroes fought and died. These men died as becomes Athenians...and you, who live, may realize the greatness of Athens and feed your eyes upon her from day to day, till love of her enfolds you and fills your hearts. By giving their lives for the State...they have enshrined themselves in our hearts and minds...for heroes have the whole earth for their tomb.

"To the parents and relations of the dead I offer comfort, not condolence....As you grow old you will be cheered by the fame of the departed....Love of honour never grows stale...and love of honour, not love of gain, warms the heart of old age."

LESSON 6. THE FATHERS OF CITIZENSHIP.

The personal appearance of Socrates as a restless old man, going about questioning people so as to make them think, is usually remembered by pupils and forms a good

s   4

introduction to the work of his pupils and followers, Plato
and Aristotle. These two philosophers must be shown as
the fathers of citizenship, the pioneers who deliberately
thought out what citizenship meant and who made a
systematic enquiry into the principles underlying community life and government. In order to make the work
attractive it must be treated biographically, lightly sketch-
ing the lives and characters of the two men, while at the
same time giving the class some conception of their ideals.
Thus Plato's two books, *The Republic* and *The Laws*, may
be analysed so as to show his ideal State and his ideal
citizens. Extracts will show that he was deeply interested
in the relations of man to right and wrong, in the policy
of States and the duties and training of citizens. Such an
outline would bring out the two great questions Plato
asked himself and his followers, viz.:

1. What is a good man and how is a man to become good?
2. What is a good State and how is a State made good?

Naturally it is impossible to do more than stimulate a
healthy curiosity, and perhaps rouse a little admiration,
that so long ago men like Plato and Aristotle could write
books which would be an eternal inspiration and guide to
all succeeding generations who are interested in the welfare
of their fellow-citizens and the good of their country. But
it is possible to give some idea of Plato's view that the
good of the State depends on the good of its citizens as a
whole and on each individual citizen as a unit; and to
emphasize the importance Plato therefore attached to
training, bringing-up, or educating the citizens of his ideal
city, so that they might become men of valour, loving the
beautiful and the virtuous, men leading just lives, keeping
their minds and bodies clean and open to the best.

Aristotle may be presented as one who was more practical-minded than Plato—a man who tried to make the best of existing cities rather than to plan ideal dream-cities. Extracts from the *Politics* will show his thirst for accurate knowledge of people and their laws; the book is the record of a searching enquiry into the existing institutions of the author's age. His ideal citizens were also men of valour and endurance, fit to defend the country, as well as men of culture leading just and temperate lives. His scheme of education can be but lightly touched on, but it can be shown how much importance he attached to training and how carefully he drew up his scheme, so that not even the diet of the children was forgotten ("plenty of milk and as little wine as possible"). Time will not permit much more than the briefest description of his ideal school; but pictures such as those in the *Schools of Hellas* may be shown and the chief subjects indicated—reading, writing, gymnastics, music, and the art of design, giving pupils some idea of what these things meant in those days. The fact that eighteen years was considered a respectable "leaving age" always impresses pupils of to-day, who are only too apt to regard ancient peoples with pity as "poor things."

CONCLUSION. Suggestions for useful exercises.

1. Ask pupils to compare Athens with any city they know in England, and then write down the names and work of the famous citizens of each city whose work is "not for an age but for all time" (*e.g.* Athens and Manchester). This exercise helps pupils to realize our debt to the Athenians better than any eulogy from the teacher or text-book. They see that we are indebted to Hellas for the beginnings of the science of numbers, of measurement, of astronomy, of hygiene and medicine; and that the Athenians left us

noble works on education and citizenship, splendid architecture and statuary, a beautiful language and an immortal literature.

2. Ask each to imagine himself elected President of the Council about the time of Pericles, and to describe his day of office.

3. Ask pupils to guess why Athens fell from her high place and write down their reasons and guesses[1]; then initiate a discussion and correct and supplement their answers and opinions—*e.g.* internal strife and class warfare; rule of demagogues; artisans no longer worked; organized as a City State yet tried to found an empire; neglected defence; general weakness and slackness; indulged almost recklessly in long and costly wars, etc. etc.

FIRST YEAR

SPRING (2ND) TERM

Syllabus (continued from previous term). Stories, largely biographical, of Rome—Legends—Romulus and Remus—Horatius—Coriolanus—The Gauls—Pyrrhus—Carthage—Hannibal—Wars—The Fall of Carthage—Roman Conquests—Pompey—Julius Caesar—Mark Antony—Cleopatra—Augustus—The Roman Empire—The Birth of Jesus Christ—Nero—Marcus Aurelius—The Eastern Empire—Justinian the Law-giver—The Barbarians and their Wanderings—The Armies of the North—The Goths—The Fall of Rome—Theodoric the Ostrogoth—The Dark Ages—The Christian Church—Great Popes.

---

[1] The guesses of pupils are often of the greatest interest (and originality); *e.g.* "It was just too good to last."

LESSONS SUGGESTED TO ILLUSTRATE
ROMAN CIVIC LIFE

1. The growth of the City State.
2. The grievances of the Plebs and the struggle for full citizenship.
3. Outline of Roman government.
4. The duties of citizens.
5. The Roman Law.
6. The decline and fall of the Roman Empire—(neglect of the duties of citizenship).

LESSON 1. THE GROWTH OF THE CITY STATE.

The class will be familiar with the traditional story of the foundation and also with the legends of early Rome from their work earlier in the term, and for our present purpose these legends are chiefly useful as an outward symbolic expression of the Roman feeling of proud and conscious unity. The Romans felt that their city was divinely founded and worthy of divine protection (compare Jupiter and Athena). It is this intense pride of their city and the community feeling to which it gave rise which must be grasped in order to understand the civic virtues of the Roman people.

The outline of Roman history will have shown pupils that the early Romans were a hardy race of people, brave and order-loving, with keen practical minds; but it can hardly be expected that without further direction pupils will have grasped that the Romans were a religious people and also a people with a keen sense of the importance of the family. These two factors played a great part in moulding the Roman character as men and as citizens, and

it is necessary to give evidence of them. Happily for the
teacher, these national characteristics are clearly reflected
and there is much suitable material.

For instance, a brief exposition of the outstanding
features of the *patria potestas* and the powers of the *paterfamilias* as the civil and religious head of the family will
explain much which, though it must seem harsh to modern
eyes, helps pupils to realize the intense family pride which
more than anything else made the Romans a great people.
Pupils will then see clearly that the family formed an *imperium in imperio*, older than the State, and that Macaulay's
description of Horatius

> facing fearful odds
> for the ashes of his fathers
> and the temples of his Gods

is most apt, because it emphasizes the two most powerful
sources of Roman patriotism and civic pride. Again, the
religious side of the early Romans is worthy of remark, for
when a Roman performed any public act (*e.g.* enrolment
as a citizen) he was also held to be doing a sacred thing.
It was natural that, as the family had its altar and was a
sacred as well as a civic community, the State should be
regarded in the same light.

The love of order and the discipline exemplified in family
life are reflected in the organization of the State and help
to account for the fact that in Rome there was more thought
about the duties of citizens than their rights or privileges
as citizens—the stern discipline of the family is reflected
in the stern demands of duty to the State. Rome was the
common father, and it is easy for pupils to see, especially
in view of the fact that the early Romans were hemmed in
with enemies—Etruscans, Latins, Gauls—that the Romans
realized this early in their history and asked themselves

" Who lives if Rome perishes ? " The common dangers, the constant struggles—first for safety then for supremacy, backed by the knowledge of the penalty of defeat (subjugation), strengthened this community-spirit and welded this collection of families into a proud, martial, and essentially practical nation.

This is the true growth of the City State which must be emphasized, and this first lesson must aim at presenting it clearly. Happily, the study of the Roman family forms an approach which is most helpful both from the view of method and of true historical appreciation.

LESSON 2. THE GRIEVANCES OF THE PLEBS AND THE STRUGGLE FOR FULL CITIZENSHIP.

In order to present this struggle clearly, it is necessary to emphasize the three chief factors which determined a man's civic standing (*caput*)—freedom, citizenship, and family rights, and to point out that the man who lost his freedom lost everything, his standing as a citizen and as a *paterfamilias*, during his captivity. If he regained it, then he recrossed the threshold of his home and the State and regained his former rights. Again, if a man lost his citizenship for wrong-doing or was transported to an island, he lost his rights; and thirdly, if he suffered a change of family, his civic rights were also affected, for by adoption he might be brought under the *potestas* of his adoptive father. Pupils can then see that civic standing meant far more to Romans than the mere right to vote; it affected his whole life—family, social, legal, and political. This throws into clear relief the grievances of the plebeians, who had the right to vote and to trade and make contracts, but were restricted in many other ways. The rule of the patricians, which began almost naturally as the guardians and legal representatives of their families, became very narrow and exclusive, and the restlessness felt by the Plebs was accentuated by the economic distress about the year 500 B.C. Once this is grasped, it is possible to formulate the grievances of the plebeians as :

1. Unable to become magistrates ;
2. Unable to hold land of their own ;
3. Unable to plead in the law courts unless backed by a patrician ;
4. Unable to marry into the patrician class ;

and to outline their claims, paying particular attention to the following :

1. Right to full citizenship.
2. Right to be secured from enslavement for debt.
3. Right to have officers of their own to look after their interests and protect them.
4. Right to a fair share of the conquered (public) lands.
5. Right to know the law.

The course and conclusion of the struggle (B.C. 509–449) may then be outlined by the pupils from their " readers " or text-books either at home or in class, the teacher contenting himself with emphasizing the length of the struggle, the shrewd common-sense shown by both parties, the orderliness and the Roman practical genius for compromise— keeping the best of the old and attaching the new. It is perhaps the only dignified " general strike " in history and forms the record of a noble struggle without bloodshed for full citizenship.

Lesson 3. Outline of Roman Government.

The aims of this lesson are firstly to give an outline of the chief assemblies and magistrates in Rome, and secondly to prepare the way for some understanding of the rights and duties of Roman citizens. If pupils have good text-books or "readers," they may be set to look up answers to questions such as the following:

What was the Senate? How was it composed? Who filled the vacancies? Was it really a law-making body? What were *senatus consulta*? To what do you attribute its great influence in the State? Name the gatherings of the Roman people: (i) the oldest, grouped in Curiae or families; (ii) the people grouped in tribes according to districts or regions in which they lived; (iii) the people grouped in classes according to wealth, as a basis for military service.

What was the gathering of the Plebs called? What were the plebeian magistrates called?

What was meant by: (i) the power of veto; (ii) the *imperium*?

What do you know about the following officers of State: The Consuls, Praetors, Tribunes, Dictator, Censor, and Pontifex Maximus?

Pupils will already be familiar with much of this work, and the lesson may then be spent firstly in testing and simplifying their knowledge, and secondly in regrouping and recasting their work, under headings such as defence, order, justice, law-making, and general administration. It will be necessary to emphasize that the Roman people were supreme—they were the State, and when gathered in their assemblies were all-powerful; but they delegated the *imperium* to the consuls, praetors, and tribunes, and gave certain of their magistrates the power to veto the acts of others. This feature of Roman government is rather puzzling to pupils at first, though later on they see that it is only another example of the shrewd common-sense and caution which characterized the Roman people.

Lesson 4. The Duties of Citizens.

Pupils will already have gathered that the first duty of a citizen was to be prepared to defend the State; and the military system by which a Roman was liable for military service between the ages of 17 and 60 years, the richer citizens as cavalry and the poorer as infantry, can be described so as to illustrate this. Secondly, the citizen's duty in helping to make laws and elect magistrates in the assemblies can be outlined; but it must be pointed out that actual law-making was rare, and the law popularly and generally meant the XII Tables (cf. Solon's code in Athens). Thirdly, the citizens' duty was to help to maintain order. In Republican Rome there were many public officers who were responsible for the order of the public places and the markets, but there was no regular police force nor armed patrols, and therefore it was the duty of every citizen to maintain order. It was in his interest; this again shows the importance of the *patria potestas*, for as the *paterfamilias* was responsible for the wrongs done by all those in his *potestas*—children, grandchildren, freedmen, and slaves— he kept very strict discipline and a careful watch over them. The Romans were an orderly people, and as a rule the extensive powers of the *paterfamilias* rendered anything equivalent to our petty sessions unnecessary until the later days of the Republic. The art of minding one's own business was thoroughly understood, as their public and private law clearly shows, and there was an almost complete absence of petty interference and restriction such as afflicts modern democracies. The Roman father kept himself and his family well in hand and saw to it that others did the same. He knew the law and he knew his rights; and perhaps this is the greatest factor which makes for order and peace in any people, then or now.

Fourthly, the Roman citizen had the duty of helping to dispense justice; he might be named to act as a judge or arbitrator, and, though unpaid, he could not refuse if his name was on the panel. If he judged wrongly or even carelessly, the Praetor who named him could hold him responsible for damages; but it is fair to assume that he almost invariably meted out justice fairly and well. This subject can be touched on again in the next lesson dealing with the Roman Law.

LESSON 5. THE ROMAN LAW.

The aim of this lesson is to give pupils some insight into the crowning and most durable legacy of the Roman people to the world and their greatest contribution to civilization. It will hardly be necessary to point out that nearly all the work they set up by force of arms has perished or left little trace, while the Roman Law stands as a monument to their love of justice, their sound common-sense, and their constructive genius[1].

From their outline of the struggle of the orders, pupils will have realized the great importance the early Romans attached to law and a knowledge of it[2]; and in this lesson it can be shown how the Romans came to know the law and why it was so important. The gradual severance of the legal administration from the College of Pontiffs, the creation of the Censor, and the publication of legal processes will also have been dealt with in discussing the magistrates and their duties.

The work of the Praetor Urbanus and his junior colleague, the Praetor Peregrinus, will also have been dealt with in Lesson 3, showing how the Praetor, though he did not make law or even admit to amending it, nevertheless in time modified it, toned down the harshness, and introduced an element of natural fairness (equity) which was often lacking in the law of a people who preferred harshness to uncertainty and vagueness. It will have shown also how, from being the state official who merely initiated legal proceedings (heard

---

[1] Cf. Napoleon in St Helena—"Nothing durable was ever set up by brute force."

[2] The XII Tables were learnt in schools; cf. learning the Ten Commandments.

complaints and then named a *judex* or arbiter), the Praetor came after hundreds of years to be a judge himself and to resemble the modern magistrate, sending out a summons, hearing evidence, and giving judgment. It will be necessary to emphasize how cautiously the Romans made changes, and to bring home clearly to pupils that it took from about 360 B.C., when the first Praetor was appointed, to about 300 A.D. for the change to be made so that the Praetor became like a modern magistrate. The effects of the absence of law reports and of newspapers will be evident; also of the absence, till fairly late in the Empire, of a professional legal class like our solicitors and barristers to-day; but it will be necessary to outline as briefly and clearly as possible how the Roman law came to be so confused that Justinian felt it essential to reduce it to an orderly statement.

In early days law-making was rare; it was not until the Empire that the Senate became a law-making body, and under the Emperor there was an enormous growth of legislation—*senatus consulta*, constitutions, edicts, rescripts, etc., which all added to the mass of laws and increased the difficulty of their interpretation.

It is easy to bring out the change from the time of the clear-cut forms of legal redress laid down by the XII Tables in the Republican days; there grew up under the Empire a vast mass of laws and the problem was to interpret them justly.

A brief mention of the work of the jurists and the learned " law interpreters " will show how their numbers had increased, so that their opinions often clashed and confusion resulted. The expedients of licensed interpreters of the law under Augustus, and later the Law of Citations in the declining years of the Empire (426), all show that the difficulty was pressing. Therefore Justinian undertook his great task.

The work of codification can be briefly outlined, mention being made of the fact that there had been previous attempts both in the Eastern and Western Empires to codify the law, but emphasis should be laid on the enormous amount of material which had to be worked through and simplified by Tribonianus and his assistants, and the wonderful zeal and energy with which they accomplished this task. (February 528 to April 529, the 1st edition; and in November 534 the 2nd edition, the source of our knowledge.)

Meanwhile Justinian had given directions for a simpler, shorter work, a sort of text-book for students, to be set in hand, and a new commission was appointed which published the *Institutes.* Extracts such as the following may be read or studied by pupils, because this gives colour and atmosphere and rounds off the lesson.

SOME EXTRACTS FROM *THE INSTITUTES OF JUSTINIAN*

The beginning

In the name of Our Lord Jesus Christ

The Emperor C. Flavius Justinian...renowned, victorious, and triumphant, ever august.

To the youth desirous of studying law:

The Imperial Majesty should be armed with laws as well as glorified with arms, that there may be good government in times of both war and peace, and the Ruler of Rome...may not only be victorious...but scrupulously regardful of justice.

Receive then these laws with eagerness of study...so...you may have ability to govern such portion of the State as may be entrusted to you.

Given at Constantinople 21st day of November in the third Consulate of the Emperor Justinian, Father of his Country,

Ever August.

From Book I, Title I.

Justice is the set and constant purpose which gives every man his due. Jurisprudence is the knowledge of things divine and human, the science of the just and the unjust.

The precepts of the law are these: to live honestly, to injure no one, and to give every man his due. The study of the law consists of two branches, law public and law private. The former relates to the welfare of the Roman State; the latter to the advantage of the individual citizen. Of private law, then, we may say that it is of three-fold origin, being collected from the precepts of nature, from those of the law of nations, or from those of the civil law of Rome.

How the Romans settled a Quarrel.

An interesting variant (or sequel) to the previous lesson would be to outline the course of an imaginary dispute between two Roman citizens, say Balbus and Marcus, and to see exactly what would have happened at various periods of Roman history. For instance, Balbus, a farmer, driving home his cows, meets one Marcus, his rival and neighbour, on a bridge. A quarrel arises and Marcus thrashes Balbus and drives one of his cows into the river, so that it is drowned.

The question now arises "How is Balbus to get redress?" Gather his sons, freedmen, and slaves and go forth against Marcus? Drive away one of Marcus' cows? Ambush and feud? Or seek legal redress (damages) and the protection of the law? It is then necessary to emphasize that ignorance of the law was not condoned by the Roman people, and as the laws dealing with "wrongs" of this class were fairly simple, the Romans had a better idea what to do than the people of most other nations. Therefore Balbus sought out the Praetor and made his complaint.

About 250 B.C.

Balbus complains in person. The Praetor commands him to bring Marcus before him; but if Marcus refuses, and Balbus cannot induce him to come or even drag him by force to the Praetor, there the matter ends; for the Romans thought "It's not the State's cow nor the Praetor's cow, but it is solely Balbus who has been wronged and it is entirely his affair." If, however, Balbus succeeded in taking Marcus by

surprise and forcing him before the Praetor, then the matter
went further. The Praetor heard the complaint, and then
appointed a judge or arbitrator from a list of suitable
citizens. This citizen was unpaid, but it was his duty as a
citizen to hear the case and decide the issues. Perhaps he
gave damages to Balbus equal to the highest value of the
dead cow and also a sum to compensate Balbus for his out-
raged feelings and black eye.

About 20 A.D.

The proceedings were practically the same, but now the
Praetor issues a summons, directing and compelling Marcus
to attend, and, as the Praetor has the *imperium*, he must
be obeyed. Therefore Marcus goes sulking to court. There
is a further advance, however, because the Praetor now not
only appoints a *judex*, or arbiter, but also sends him a little
brief, or note, telling him what he has to decide. This was
a great advance and was welcome, after the original distrust
of anything new had worn off. Then the matter goes as
before.

About 250 A.D.

A similar dispute arises, and now Balbus goes in person and
complains to the Praetor as before. The latter issues a summons and Marcus attends on the appointed day. But now
there is a great change. The Praetor hears the whole case
himself and gives judgment. This is much quicker and less
formal; it is a welcome advance, for the Praetor by this time
resembles our modern magistrate or county court judge, who
grants a summons, hears the case, and gives judgment,
without any jury or arbitration.

A simple example like this teaches its own lessons, but
it will be necessary to point out that "going to law" then

(as now) was full of pit-falls. The old Roman Balbus the First (250 B.C.) had to be very careful, for if he made a slip in stating his case, either in words or actions, he might lose it, as the XII Tables had made very strict rules for actions. The pantomime aspect of these early legal dramas can be shown by saying that in all probability Balbus would be expected to bring the head, or even the carcase, of the dead cow into court, and to show his bruises as evidence of his loss and hurt. This shows pupils the formal aspect of early law. The lesson ought to bring out the fact that then, as now, ignorance of the law was no excuse and that it was the duty of every citizen to play his part, for there was no such thing as sending a deputy. "Going to law" was, like all other duties of Roman citizens, a direct personal obligation, which could not be passed on[1].

LESSON 6. THE DECLINE AND FALL OF THE ROMAN EMPIRE, showing the results of neglecting the duties of citizenship.

This lesson cannot possibly do more than point out some of the outstanding causes of the decay, but it can stimulate thought. Pupils will be familiar with the armies of the North, the Barbarians, their restless wanderings and frequent descents upon the Empire in the third and fourth centuries. Their attention will also have been called to the growth of piracy in the Mediterranean and the results of this on the overcrowded city of Rome. A rough map

[1] For schools where Latin is taught on the direct method, the history and Latin masters might collaborate to write a Latin playlet based on the *sacramentum*—say, a case dealing with dispute as to the ownership of a slave. The lively pantomime and mock combat aspect of this would make an instant appeal and both the history and Latin courses would benefit. (See Hunter, *Introduction to Roman Law*, p. 198.)

showing the trade routes, and particularly those along which grain and food were carried, will show this clearly and save much explanation. By means of examples it can be shown that the Romans no longer worked as they used to do; they were dependent for their food and very existence on the provinces of the Empire. Therefore their neglect of the first duty of citizens, to be ready and prepared to defend the Empire, was fatal neglect[1]. Not only did they become dependent on hired barbarian armies, but they neglected sea power; and so the Vandals had a much easier task than the Goths and other enemies on land, for when they attacked Rome they cut across her "lines of communication" in the Mediterranean, captured Rome, and for a fortnight despoiled the city. The extravagance of the ruling classes in Rome and the greed of the later governors and Caesars resulted in excessive taxation, which drained the provinces and crushed out of existence the well-to-do freemen and small farmers, who formed the sober middle class, the backbone of the state. The greed of the colossal, meddlesome, and expensive horde of corrupt, inefficient, civil servants, which had grown up and which battened on the Empire, killed private enterprise. The excesses of the mob in Rome, which no longer worked and had become largely dependent on doles for its existence and on public games for its amusement, formed yet another cause of decay. In short, the ruling classes no longer ruled and the people no longer worked[2]. It is easily grasped by the class that there was a complete neglect of the duties of citizenship, and as the Romans for a long period had refused to grant the provincial peoples the full standing of citizens, by the time of the

---

[1] Compare the *personnel* of a legion in the reign of Augustus with that of the time of Honorius.

[2] The absence of any outstanding manufacture or industry was remarkable in so populous a city.

earliest Saxon attacks against England, when the Barbarians were becoming most daring and reckless, the Empire had become an unwieldy, ramshackle collection of administrative units. It was too vast; and as in the provinces national spirit and a strong sense of unity was growing up, and the "administrative units" were becoming nations with kings and ideals of citizenship and self-government of their own[1], it is easy for pupils to realize why the Empire crumbled in the West.

NOTES ON METHOD.

The above outlines indicate the subject-matter of the talks on Greek and Roman citizenship. They are very inadequate in so far as they give the reader the impression that the pupils' share in the work is merely that of listening to the teacher. Certainly in a great deal of the instruction it must take the form of matter "told to the children," and to a large extent their share in the work must be merely listening; but, in actual teaching, the lessons will be quickened by lively questioning and frequent reference to to-day.

From the beginning of the course the pupils ought to be taught to distinguish between questions which call for the application of common-sense and intelligence—"questions of intelligence"—and questions which cannot be answered without a knowledge of facts—"questions of fact," and should be encouraged to regard it as a point of honour to

[1] These States must be shown as "people-groups," bound by the strongest ties of family and common ideals. It is not too early to emphasize that it was not altogether geography or race which settled (though they sensibly affected) the foundation of States. The State is the big family group of common ideals, and its citizens have "father duties"—defence, law and order, etc.—and "mother duties," peace-making, dealing justice, settling disputes, etc. (cf. the "strong arm of the law"; yet justice is always regarded as a woman, "mild and even-handed").

attempt to answer a "question of intelligence." In the same way they must be encouraged to admit ignorance or failure to understand what is being taught, because that saves time and is straightforward. To induce a class to adopt this attitude takes time, because, if the class feeling is with the teacher, and if they like or respect him, then there is a tendency to pretend that they follow. They will appear interested and look as if they grasped what is being told them. In this way the very qualities which are valuable assets in teaching are really telling against the efficiency of the instruction, because a teacher proceeds with the lesson and thinks all is well, until some pupil asks a question which shows that he (and usually others) have not grasped some essential point. Therefore unless every effort is made to get the class to be perfectly frank with the teacher, unless he regards himself as the class leader, it is very difficult— indeed almost impossible—to make these lessons successful.

FIRST YEAR

SUMMER (3RD) TERM

Syllabus. Stories of the Middle Ages, the Discovery of New Worlds, and the Awakening of Europe, based on reading, largely biographical[1].

During this term the chief aim of the teaching is to cover the ground and to give continuity and coherence to the reading. With so wide and varied a syllabus there is no call for any special lessons devoted to the civic aspect of history, although pupils will naturally see the working

---

[1] Such books as *The Discovery of New Worlds* and *The Awakening of Europe* by M. B. Synge (Blackwood) or *Heroes of European History* by Louise Creighton (Longman), or for older pupils *Introduction to World History* by Keatinge and Frazer (Black) and many other books are suitable.

of such principles as that the presence of a foreign enemy
in the territory of a country tends to give rise to a spirit
of nationality in the oppressed people—*e.g.* the Moors in
Spain, the English in France, and the Spanish in the
Netherlands. But in this term, with so wide a field of
survey, it is well to rely on rapid reading, letting history
tell its own story, to give pupils a background for their
future work, so as to link up the stories of European history
with the deeper study of English history in succeeding
years.

SECOND YEAR

1. AUTUMN TERM. Outlines of English History to 1066 A.D.
2. SPRING TERM. Outlines of English History, 1066 to
   1485 A.D.
3. SUMMER TERM. Social and Industrial History—Life in
   the Middle Ages.

AUTUMN (1ST) TERM

PERIOD—*Outline of History of England to* 1066 A.D. (20
  periods).

LESSONS SUGGESTED (5 periods).

1. Introductory Lesson: Communities and their Government.
2. The Government of our Ancestors—the English
   before they came to Britain.
3 & 4. Anglo-Saxon Government in Britain, showing the
   outlines of our national system.
5. Revision lesson, showing the rights and duties of
   freemen.

LESSON 1. COMMUNITIES AND THEIR GOVERNMENT.

The method and the amount of detail in this lesson will vary with the age and attainment of the class, but for children of about 12 to 13 years of age the best starting-point is the community they know most intimately—their own family.

The children all see that they have much in common with their brothers and sisters—they live together, eat together, have the same feelings about things, feel proud if a brother, sister, or parent does something creditable or worthy, are concerned for each other's health and safety and welfare, and have more or less the same ideals. This idea of having common interests and ideals is the starting-point and is very important in the following lessons; it explains the key-word " Community."

From this the rules which govern family life or community life can be deduced and general truths about people having common interests and living together in peace enunciated. Thus pupils will see that in a well-ordered family :

(1) *All help to defend the home, e.g.* in case of attack by unruly neighbours, evil-disposed persons, thieves, fire, etc.

(2) *Order must be kept* in the home, though quarrels arise even in the best families. How ? By a general desire to keep order and prevent trouble. Importance of this mutual agreement, which is the sign of a well-ordered family, the members of which rarely have to appeal to their parents to settle matters or quell disorder. But if one, in defiance of general wishes, is a nuisance, resort to power and punishment rests with father or mother, who is really head of community and from whom there is no appeal—*e.g.* father says "Can't go—that settles it." Breaking this decision leads to disorder and punishment, for in

every community there must be someone vested with the *imperium* (cf. Rome).

(3) *Disputes must be settled.* See above—either among themselves or by appeal to parent, who arbitrates and is the final court. His decision may often leave a feeling of resentment, but must be "put up with," because it is the will of the family as expressed by its chief.

(4) *Rules must be drawn up*, to prevent disputes continually arising and to ensure safety of family. The class will supply examples showing that family rules are nearly always customs and unwritten laws.

These four main rules having been deduced, they can be summarized under heads of: (i) Defence, (ii) Order, (iii) Justice, (iv) Laws. It is an easy step towards the application and study of these headings in a larger community.

The lessons may be rounded off by briefly stating whose business it is in the State to attend to these functions of government to-day, *e.g.*

Duties	How carried out
1. Defence.	All citizens ready and willing; but regular soldiers and sailors specially kept and trained for instant readiness.
2. Order.	All citizens responsible and must help; but policemen specially trained and always ready.
3. Justice.	All citizens, as jurymen or as witnesses on oath, or if appointed as unpaid Justices of the Peace; but magistrates and judges specially paid and appointed to administer difficult law.
4. Laws.	All citizens, as represented by Parliament, which makes statutes of the realm and imposes and regulates taxes. All citizens, by their representatives in the local Councils—District, Town, City, or County (Bye-laws).

The latter portion of the lesson may conveniently be given as home-work, as it requires independent work and will tend to drive home what has been learnt in class.

With older children the community considered in class might be their city or town, *e.g.* its pride as a city—best football team, best recruiting during the war, best Housing Bonds etc. But the method of taking the lesson remains very similar to the above outline.

Again, older pupils may have the four headings (Defence etc.) given out to them, and, if they are provided with " source books " or documents, may be asked to show how the Anglo-Saxon peoples in England governed themselves, arranging their answers under the four headings. This would be very suitable for two lessons in class and two "preparations." A lesson could then be spent in class amplifying and correcting their efforts.

But for the majority of classes, it will be found that a prepared lesson from the teacher is necessary in the early stages. Whatever method is found most suitable, it must clearly show that the specialists (paid or unpaid)—soldiers, policemen, magistrates, and judges—have been appointed to help, but the duties of all citizens remain the same and are essential to the health and well-being of the State.

LESSON 2. THE GOVERNMENT OF OUR EARLY ANCESTORS.

This lesson aims at giving pupils some description of the North German tribes, particularly with reference to their character and their ideas of self-government, as described by Tacitus. Extracts from the *Germania* will show best that they were a free and rather easy-going people, when not at war, respecting women-folk, disliking towns or city life, fond of the open air, hunting, and sport. They usually lived in little clusters of families, but it is possible to trace three chief groups : (i) The *vicus* ("wic," "wich"), a group of neighbours, which became the township (and sometimes the parish) later on when these people settled in Britain.

(ii) A larger group called by Tacitus the *pagus*, which developed into the *Hundred*, a most useful fighting group of kinsmen, self-judging and self-governing. It will be seen later that King Alfred used this group for his " fyrd," or militia, and King Edgar used it for purposes of justice, law, and order—the Hundred Court. (iii) A still larger group, the tribe, which was practically the people or the nation, and when assembled as "the Folk" was the sovereign people. The simple quotation "On less important matters the chiefs deliberate, on more important the whole tribe" throws a flood of light on the customs of the people and on their moots, and leads the way to some consideration of the chiefs and their importance.

Chiefs with authority to persuade rather than power to command.

These chiefs must be shown as the leaders in war and peace who formed a nobility, their rank gained by service and work ; they were the *Comites* ; and in England they became the land-owners and the right worthy " thegns." They formed the basis of the army, a sort of select corps, always ready at short notice and able to train the "tender-foot" when the people went to war. They became the leaders in peace and were gradually appealed to by lesser men to settle disputes. The chief leaders gathered a band of these trusty warriors around them ; they became their body-guards and their councils, but always remained sworn blood-brothers rather than dependents (cf. Beowulf).

After a lesson exemplifying points like the above, it is easy for pupils to realize why, when these peoples crossed to Britain, they were almost at once little nations, and why it took so long for them to settle down together as one people. Further it will help them to appreciate the strong community-feeling of the folk.

LESSONS 3 AND 4. ANGLO-SAXON GOVERNMENT, SHOWING THE
OUTLINES OF OUR NATIONAL SYSTEM.

The lessons fall naturally under the four headings already outlined:

1. How the Anglo-Saxons defended themselves.
2. How they kept order.
3. How they judged and settled disputes.
4. How they drew up laws to avoid strife and disorder, etc.

In order to exemplify these points it will be necessary to describe:

1. *The defence of the country*, pointing out that the army was the people in arms (refer to the fyrd in Alfred's day), showing how it was "called up" and who fought. A consideration of Alfred's ships as the germ of our fleet and the importance of sea communication will show the danger and difficulty of land travel and transport.

2. *The system for maintaining law and order.* Pupils will be familiar with the blood-feud, due to the lack of strong authority; and the lesson must show how very gradually the idea of disorder as undesirable grew up. A few concrete examples of blood-money (*wergeld* or "mangold") will help to emphasize the feeling about crime and disorder, showing that in Saxon times quite a tariff of crimes and prices grew up: *e.g.* killing a Ceorl, 200 shillings; a Welchman, 100 shillings; an Earl, 4800 shillings; an Archbishop, 9000 shillings; the King, 18,000 shillings. In fact, all were too dear to kill, though there was no idea that to kill injured anyone other than the slain and his dependents, and it was only gradually that killing or assaulting came to be regarded as a crime against the community; and with this came the idea of the "King's Peace." It is necessary to emphasize the co-operative aspect of keeping order derived from the open field system of farming, which made co-operation essential, *e.g.* sharing ploughs and teams of oxen, etc. This gave rise

to frequent meetings to arrange things and to settle disputes, which in the absence of written rules were frequent, although custom was strong and the elders generally knew what was customary. It is easy for pupils to see that these meetings became early courts, where men settled disputes —cattle-stealing, assaults, moving boundary marks, etc. Again, the importance of the tythings as little groups of families must be emphasized (refer to lessons on Early Rome). Extracts from the Saxon laws will be found the greatest help; they are the best illustrations and by their directness and simplicity make an instant appeal to pupils. For instance, the laws of King Edgar which roughly defined the procedure of the Hundred Court are remarkably clear— " First, they shall gather themselves once in four weeks... Second, they shall ride forth after thieves. Every tything man and all men shall raise the hue and cry and hand over the thief to justice." Also, " If any man shall put difficulties in the way of the Hundred Court or refuse its verdict he shall pay thirty pennies...etc." Again, the laws of Athelstan (925–940) supply many illustrations of early police measures, *e.g.* " Every landless man must have a lord...one must be found for him "; and " Every man must respect his neighbour's burgh or enclosure," which shows that from the earliest times the Englishman's home, however humble, has been regarded as his castle (*e.g.* fines for trespass on the King's property — King's burghbryce, 120 shillings; breaking a ceorl's hedge, 5 shillings). The gradual rise and extension of the King's Peace is well illustrated by the law of Edmund: " If any man seeks refuge in my burgh or in a church...and anyone hereafter assault him, he who does this shall be liable...," which shows pupils that the King was beginning to regard towns and churches, and later high roads, as under his special protection and care.

3. *How justice was dealt and disputes settled.* A brief description of the local moots will show how in these meetings the folk themselves decided what should be done in the neighbourhood—how a road was to be made or repaired, or a thief caught, or a tax raised; and that, when sitting in judgment, the moot became the court of the neighbourhood and the neighbours were thus the witnesses, the oathmen (witnesses as to character), and also the jury and judges. In the earliest times all men's oaths were equal; later on the value of evidence or oath, like the " wer," depended on the amount of land a man held, as this usually determined his rank, *e.g.* " A King's retainer if he be a communicant may swear for 60 hides " (Law of Ine of Wessex).

4. *The making of the laws.* It must be pointed out that for practical purposes nearly all law was the custom of the neighbourhood. There was very little written law; the few laws necessary were made by the King on the advice of the Witan. Pupils easily regard the Witan as a folkmote, but an example like the following will show them its true composition: Witan held at Luton in the year 931, at which were present: two archbishops, two Welsh princes, seventeen bishops, five ealdormen, five abbots, and fifty-nine ministri (thegns). These counsellors really " backed up " the King in the making of laws and ordinances; they also witnessed and approved grants of land, and also grants of the right of holding a court, which, after Canute's time, usually went as a matter of course with the grant of land.

LESSON 5. REVISION.

Points to be noticed in Anglo-Saxon Government. No rights without duties and obligations, *e.g.* the freeman had a voice in the government, but was obliged to fight to defend the country and help to maintain order, attend courts, uphold and abide by judgment of his neighbours, help to repair roads, etc.—in short, play his part and share all the obligations of freemanship. The same applied to the ealdorman, for, although he was the chief man in the shire, yet he had many exàcting duties, *e.g.* to raise and train the levy, and to report and suppress disorder. Also he was expected to summon the more important courts and superintend their working. In fact, land-owning (better " holding ") gave privileges and rank, but entailed definite duties and obligations.

Therefore all from highest to lowest had very strict obligations, which were often settled and defined by custom. The land was poor, farming was difficult, and all had to work very hard indeed—really by the sweat of their brows, and at times with the " wolf" actually clawing at their doors.

Instead of freemen of pure blood being equal to any in the land, by the time of Edward the Confessor the possession of land has become the visible and material sign of freedom —of being a freeman. Men with little or no land were becoming dependent on prosperous men with more land. The fyrd had become the gathering of land-owners in arms, the courts, the courts of land-owners. Grants of land also often granted the right to hold a court, until at last a landless man was looked upon with suspicion. Thus small people gained protection, richer people gained power ; but the possession of land was becoming all-important and the way was paved for the Norman system of feudalism, and also for the earliest and simplest form of representation.

The vast importance of local government, the meetings in the village, co-operative farming, also joining together for police work, for dispensing justice, for raising taxes, for repairing roads, all these are points for notice. In fact, if we wish to seek out the germs of our freedom and the ways in which the English in English government have combined the greatest freedom with the least restraint, we must seek them in the local government of our old English towns and villages.

SECOND YEAR

SPRING (2ND) TERM

PERIOD—*History of England,* 1066 *to* 1485.

From the syllabus it will be seen that the period contains a number of topics which call for detailed treatment and concrete example and illustration: Feudalism—the settlement after the Conquest—the Church and Crown—the rise of a strong central government—the Crusades—Henry II and the coming of the Friars—John and Magna Carta—the beginnings of Parliament—Edward I and the war with France.

It will be found helpful if the outline of history is given in this term and the social history treated in the next term (Summer), because the work of the third term then throws much light on the work of the foregoing terms, and gives the teacher scope for revision and opportunity to amplify and illustrate the topics treated earlier in the year. Therefore during this term the function of history in the indirect teaching of citizenship consists to a great extent in showing:

(i) The development of national unity.
(ii) The development of the central government.
(iii) The rise and development of royal justice and law.
(iv) The birth and development of the idea of representation and the beginnings of Parliament.

Every opportunity should be taken to point out and to illustrate these developments as they arise, without giving an undue constitutional bias to the instruction. There are many examples where these points can be emphasized without special lessons. For instance, such matters as the growing sense of national unity, and the need for representation in government as the units of administrative government became larger and the difficulties which the freemen had to overcome in attending the shire courts became greater, are only thrown into true perspective if the pupils realize the topography of England in the eleventh and twelfth centuries and onwards—the dense forests, swamps, and marshes, and the bad roads. The wolves alone in many parts of the country were enough to make a journey of even ten miles more hazardous than any journey to-day. The march of Harold the Saxon from Yorkshire to Senlac in three weeks might well have been accounted wonderful, and to emphasize points like these shows clearly the natural forces in England which encouraged strong local feelings, almost clannish in intensity, and militated against national unity or the centralization of government.

For the purpose of tracing the development of ordered government and national unity we are chiefly concerned with William's work as an administrator in developing the machinery of government.

Again, regarding the matter from the standpoint of the Conqueror himself, let the class note in their books as below :

HINDERING FACTORS	HELPING FACTORS
Forces in England working for disorder and making William's task of centralization very difficult:	Useful instruments of government which William found here:
(1) *Natural features*—swamps, forests, bad roads, and general difficulty of travel.	(1) Land already parcelled out into manors, with little manor courts—few or no landless men. Facts of Feudalism already in England when William began his conquest.

(2) *Barons* who were great land-holders and great feudal lords, semi-independent, like their fathers in Normandy; who all held land (tenants), and who all held courts to judge their tenants (sub-tenants).

(2) *Sheriffs* in shires, and Reeves in towns will be useful as royal officers, and William can make them *his* agents.

(3) *Local courts*—stronghold of freeholders:
1. Courts of the townships.
2. Hundred courts.
3. Shire courts.

(4) *The Norman system of Sworn Inquiry*—Inquest—Evidence on Oath.

A lesson on these lines clears up much of the doubt in pupils' minds, because they begin to see the task as it presented itself to William. Where could William look for help in settling and governing England? The class will remember that he had the services of:

(i) Trusty officers of his household: steward (head reeve of Royal estates), butler, constable; (ii) The great officers of State: justiciar, treasurer, marshal, chancellor; (iii) The Great Council (*Magnum Concilium*) which usually met three times a year at Winchester, Westminster, and Gloucester. If in great straits, then the King called his Great Council together to " back him up."

It will be seen that, by the end of his reign, William had imposed his peace and his will on a reluctant people and an unruly baronage. He had begun to build up the machinery of the central government, aided by his smaller council of trusty advisers. His work was developed by Henry I, Henry II, and Edward I; but William laid the foundations with no mean skill, retaining and making use of much that was best in Saxon government (*T.R.E.*)[1], remoulding it and adding discipline, orderliness, and unity, the grandest features of Norman government, without which the older

[1] Temp. Ed. Regis, *sc.* Edward the Confessor.

Anglo-Saxon ideas of freedom might have perished in baronial anarchy and disorder.

In dealing with the reign of Henry II it is difficult to give any account of his reforms and the policy which furthered the work of William I, and developed the rise of a central government, in terms simple enough for the pupils to understand. The reforms of Henry II call for a strong introduction of the personal element, and it is worth while to spend a lesson or part of a lesson trying to picture Henry of Anjou as a man. He was a wonderful personality, and his birth and position gave him the utmost scope for his powers. He was not merely Duke Henry, as his grandfather had been Duke William, but he was King of England and ruler of the largest Empire in Christendom. His writs and commands were enforced from the South of France to the borders of Scotland, and it is fortunate for the teacher that there are excellent descriptions of Henry of Anjou extant, for the interest of the class is easily aroused and held by the appearance and personality of the King. The class soon knows the man and realizes the aims of his policy and the difficulties he surmounted, and pupils can be set to work out from their text-books what Henry did for the administration of justice, legal and judicial reform, the keeping of order, police measures, the defence of the country, and military measures.

If the text-book is very inadequate, it might be more useful for the teacher to give a set lesson first and let the class summarize it for home-work revision, as the teacher can present the matter much more clearly than the text-books, because he is alive and he knows his class. For instance, in dealing with Henry's work for justice, a table like the following is most helpful :

COURTS OF JUSTICE IN HENRY'S REIGN

1. *Feudal courts.* Courts of the Manor: court leet, court baron, court customary.

2. *Local courts.* Courts of the township (presided over by the reeve), the hundred, and the shire.

3. *Royal courts.* At first only the most important of the feudal courts; these latter became all-powerful and gradually superseded the baronial (feudal) courts.

   N.B. All the above courts were gradually brought under the direction of the King and his Great Council, which became the supreme court of justice. Its committees became courts as well as departments of state, *e.g.* Exchequer, Curia Regis, King's Bench.

4. *Church courts.* To try clerks: the courts of the bishop or abbot.

HENRY'S AIMS

1. To diminish the power of the barons by reducing their powers of dispensing justice and weakening their courts by:

   (i) Taking away their suitors (causing the barons to lose suit) and attracting clients to his own courts by means of writs, by which the grieved party, injured or dispossessed, applied to the King for a written order. This forced the baron to have the case tried in the royal court;

   (ii) denying the power of the barons to try criminal cases and making crimes pleas of the Crown;

   (iii) sending the judges round to the shire courts at regular intervals;

   (iv) offering a better chance of getting justice in his courts than prevailed in the baronial courts, by use of juries—cf. old Norman inquest used in the Doomsday. The same principle was applied to justice, both for criminal offences (jury of presentment) and also for civil actions, *e.g.* disputes about land, etc.

2. To reorganize the defence of the country, so as to be more independent of the feudal levies of the barons.

   Note (i) Scutage—honourable money payment in lieu of military service.

   (ii) Assize of Arms—every freeman, because he is a freeman, to bear arms according to his rank and station in life, so as to be prepared.

   (iii) Castles to be garrisoned by the King's officers (Constables).

s   6

This lesson of itself will not be very useful unless it
makes the pupils realize how the barons must have felt
and how they must have longed for the bad old times, or,
as they would have said, the good old times of Stephen's
reign, when might and the dungeon overshadowed right;
and how they must have loathed " this upstart Angevin,"
spoiling " fun " with his writs and his justices and prying
sheriffs! On the other hand, the pupils realize that the
reign marks the beginning of the King's Peace, and the
justice delivered in the King's court and the shire courts
(when the Sheriff or justice was presiding) is no longer the
judgment or law of Duke William, but the judgment and
law of England—laws and rules which had their beginnings
in old Saxon custom and which have grown up with England.
Freemen gained benefits or rights, but they also assumed
duties and responsibilities. Hence law and order gained the
respect and support of all " good men and true," and with
the common law grew a common love for England. England
as a nation was coming into being.

Magna Carta

Perhaps more nonsense has been written, and is still
taught, about Magna Carta than about any other document or event in history; and if pupils in secondary schools
are to be taught anything beyond the name and date of
the Charter, if it is to mean anything to them, then it is
necessary for them to understand how the King got his
money and revenue in the thirteenth century—and, in fact,
for long after. In all probability taxation and representation grew up hand in hand, and the rise of Parliament, and
in later times its supremacy in the system of government,
depended to a great extent on its control over money
matters. Therefore it seems essential that a lesson—it

might almost be regarded as a "key" lesson—should be given on this subject, so that pupils may apply the knowledge they have gained to work on the Charter.

A suggestive exercise is to ask the class to index the more important clauses in the following way:

Assuming that the pupils have each a copy of the Charter in their "documents," the teacher need only introduce the Charter quite briefly, showing how John had offended the barons, the clergy, and the traders of the towns, how he had "bled" the Jews, and how his defeat at Bouvines and consequent demands for further aids and taxation brought matters to a crisis. The result was the Charter—really a treaty of peace between the King and the baronage and Church (one can hardly say the nation without giving the pupils a wrong impression). The clauses outline the conditions of peace (or better, armistice) thrust on the King by the baronial forces. Without further comment or criticism, ask pupils to index it clause by clause as on p. 84, so giving them an opportunity for independent work.

This exercise gives pupils scope for independent work ; it makes them think ; and they see that Magna Carta embodied little that was new. It was vague and indefinite on many important points, but pupils realize the importance of having "something in black and white," to which the King could be held. They also realize that the barons themselves showed, by the elaborate precautions they took to enforce the treaty of peace, that they expected the King to break his oath—hence twenty-six barons were given the right to revolt in order to uphold the Charter. *Quis custodiet ipsos custodes?* Although much more has since been read into the Charter than even the exultant barons ever intended, it became a monument, a landmark on the road of constitutional development and freedom. It

Clause	Central idea	Cui bono?	Remarks (e.g. abuse it was intended to prevent or reasons for its insertion)
1	(i) Holy Church to be free and its privileges respected (ii) General promise of unwritten liberties	The Church ...	Rufus, Henry II, Richard I (Hugh of Lincoln), and John had depressed the Church. Sees had been kept vacant and income pocketed by the Kings
2	Reliefs defined and fixed ...	Barons	To prevent unjust and arbitrary reliefs being taken
3	Wardship	Barons	To prevent the King plundering the estates of minors and widows
12	Fixing aids and scutage and defining their purpose	Barons, Knights, City of London	General promise not to take aids except by consent
14	Convening Great Council ...	Greater Tenants and Clergy	Common counsel of realm for the purpose of assessing an aid
20	Fines	Freemen, Villagers, Traders, Merchants	
21	Trials	Barons	Trial by peers (equals) not by a royal judge
34	Barons' private courts	Barons	The King must not evoke cases from the Lords' courts by his writ to the Royal courts
39	Justice	All freemen ...	Just trial by law, none to be imprisoned or dispossessed without trial
40	Justice	All freemen ...	Justice not to be sold (a splendid promise!)
41	Trade	Merchants ...	To be free from evil tolls and exactions; foreigners to be regarded as hostages
45	Forest	Probably all who lived near forests	Twelve *sworn* men (knights) of the same county... inquest...to correct evil customs
52	General promise of restitution and amendment	All freemen ...	General promise

was issued and reissued many times and became to English freemen, knights and barons of the Middle Ages almost what the Twelve Tables were to the ancient Romans. If the barons could have spoken with one voice, as they returned with their followers to the manors on the demobilization of the army, they would probably have said " Well, whatever happens now, we've got that ! "—though some of the more unruly spirits might have said " Well, whatever happens to the Charter, we've dished the King ! "

THE GROWTH OF PARLIAMENT

With older pupils a most useful exercise is to set them to trace out the growth of representation and taxation, showing how they grew up together. Using their text-books and documents, they would be able to write down a summary such as the following, though the amount of detail would depend very largely on the text-books and documents at their disposal, and the teacher would be quite satisfied if the more important stages, viz. the election of juries in 1194, the crisis of 1213, De Montfort's Parliament of 1265, and the Model Parliament were remembered ; because this shows quite satisfactorily how the feudal assembly of 1213 developed into the Parliament of 1295—an assembly representing those who pray, who fight, and who labour : Clergy, Lords, and Commons.

TAXATION AND REPRESENTATION (1216–1296)

The whole system of trial by jury implies representation—the person tried is judged by the neighbourhood ; for the voice of the jury was the verdict of the country-side (neighbours). Early each hundred and township was represented by representatives not necessarily elected, but "speaking for" their district.

1194. Juries elected. Four knights in each shire, who chose two knights in each hundred, who in turn chose ten more, making twelve, who formed the jury of the hundred. This is the jury of presentment.

1194. Coroners elected to keep pleas of the Crown.

1213.   As the result of the crisis four lawful men and the reeve from the royal demesne were summoned to meet the King; and in the same year four discreet men from each county were summoned to treat concerning the business of the country (*ad loquendum nobiscum...*).

1225.   Charters reissued for an "aid" assessed by four men elected in each county.

1232.   Four men and reeve elected to assess the one-fortieth.

1237.   Four knights and a clerk elected to assess the thirteenth.

1254.   Regent summoned four knights from each county to see "what aid they will grant to us in this our great necessity," as the King was in great straits in Gascony and heavily engaged.

1265.   *Famous Parliament* called by Simon de Montfort, to which were summoned the bishops and barons, and in addition two knights of the shire and *two representatives of certain cities and boroughs*. This Parliament formed a precedent which was not always acted upon.

1267.   Statute of Marlborough, "Enacted by the discreet men of our Kingdom both greater and lesser."

1273.   Great oath-swearing assembly: four knights from each shire, four citizens from certain cities, archbishops, bishops, earls, and barons.

1295.   *The Model Parliament*, at which were present: Archbishops (2), abbots and all the bishops (72), archdeacons (2), proctors from each diocese (one for cathedral clergy and one for other clergy); these summoned by the "faith and love" they bore the King. Earls (7 or 8), barons (41), summoned by name by the "faith and hommage" they bore the King, two knights from each shire (74 in all), two citizens from each city (220 in all).

These were summoned by the King "to treat, ordain and *execute* (*ad faciendum*)," and this assembly was no longer a body called to ratify the King's will or his acts (merely to "back up" the King and his ministers) but a body to which the King might have said "What are you going to *do* about it?" This assembly is a Parliament. It makes statutes. It represents the States of the Realm and speaks for the Estates of England. The *imperium* has not left the hands of the King and his magnates, but a precedent had been established for all time and Parliament had come to stay—and this Parliament of 1295 was a veritable national assembly representing all sorts and conditions of men. How the representatives were elected is not clear, but the important thing is that long before the other States of Europe had evolved any method of expressing and representing the will of the nation, the English people had evolved a model Parliament which spoke for the nation and embodied the principle that what touches all shall be ordained by all.

The foregoing summary might not unreasonably be expected from pupils in the second or third years of secondary schools. If, however, such an exercise is felt to be too difficult, it would be wiser to view the constitutional development of the period quite briefly but vividly from the three points—John and Magna Carta, De Montfort and his Parliament, and Edward I and the Model Parliament. The matter should be treated in a more biographical manner, because this is especially suitable and effective in the case of Edward I, who in 1295 was like the British lion at bay, and whose appeal to the nation in that year, if, properly presented to a class to-day, probably arouses more interest and certainly more enthusiasm than it did in the breasts of the heavily taxed " fellows of this realm " who were so "strictly enjoined to be present in person at Westminster" in November, 1295.

From this date, it is possible to direct the attention of the class to the next stage in the development of Parliament and to ask them to be on the look-out for advances in its power and to notice the claim of the representatives in Parliament assembled not only to grant taxes but to have a voice in the spending of them ; to have the right to call to account and to punish the King's ministers if they break the Statute law (*e.g.* the Good Parliament) ; to regain and enforce the old right, which the Witan possessed, that in the event of a disputed or doubtful succession, Parliament could decide the succession (refer to Henry IV, Henry VII, and Henry VIII, Act of Succession), and in times of national crisis even to remove and depose the King.

Beyond work on these lines, it is hardly possible or desirable to go with pupils under fifteen years of age, because the subject-matter is too difficult. Thus the constitutional experiments of the reign of Henry III, though full of interest to teachers as students of constitutional history, are unsuitable for school history and outside its content. But it must be noted that throughout the whole period the claims and power of Parliament were growing, and it was slowly establishing its claim to exercise a general, though ill-defined, supervision of the government of England. The short but important life of the Good Parliament (1376) may be pointed out, as showing the increasing importance of the Knights of the Shire, the expression of the principle " No grants until grievances have been redressed," and the rise of control of the King's ministers, *e.g.* impeachment of Latimer as " useless to the King and kingdom."

This period gives the teacher an opportunity of pointing out not only the restrictions of the royal power, but the growth of that loyalty to the Sovereign which has been so remarkable in our history. To account for this would go too deeply into traits in the national character and the personal attributes and policy of our Kings, but, as the occasion arises, it is well to point out that in England the King has always been regarded as the supreme giver of justice and the fountain of mercy—almost as the father of his country. This is clearly shown by the expressions of the leaders of the revolts of the lower orders—it was usually the "wicked ministers" they blamed; and there must have been an abiding respect for kingship, based partly on tradition and partly on experience, for the idea of the " rebels " seemed to have been " If only we can see the King, he will do justice and grant us relief" (*vide* Peasants' Revolt, Wat Tyler's rebellion, and even the Pilgrimage of Grace). This belief was often misplaced, as in the last example, but it shows that the commons had a genuine belief in the goodness and beneficent intention of the sovereign lord towards his people, which has always been a feature of Merrie England (especially under Elizabeth), and which has caused the person and office of the King or Queen to be enshrined in the hearts of the people as a symbol of the majesty and greatness of the nation itself. This is why loyalty and devotion to the King to-day mean to patriotic Englishmen very much what devotion to "la Patrie" means to patriotic Frenchmen. Froissart and the *Chronicles* afford many striking passages showing how the nation looked to the King for guidance and help. Edward I, Edward III, and Henry V all illustrate this spirit of loyalty. Pride of the King was pride in England, and devotion to the leader fostered that spirit of comradeship and unity among those he led which distinguishes a nation from a collection of persons.

SECOND YEAR

SUMMER (3RD) TERM

Social and Industrial History, 1066 to 1485.

It will be observed that the social aspects of the period have been reserved for the third term's work, and one of the outstanding merits of this arrangement is that it enables far greater attention to be given to local history than would otherwise have been possible, without interfering with the continuity of the political aspect of the period.

Supposing the term to be of about ten to twelve weeks' duration, this will allow not less than twenty lessons (if only two per week are allotted to history) and at least ten (in some cases twenty) periods of home-work or preparation for the subject. In this number of lessons it is possible to treat the chosen topics with enough detail and care to make them really useful and enjoyable.

As the syllabus practically covers the social life of the Middle Ages, it teems with topics of the greatest interest; and naturally, with so many topics to be treated in a term, examples must be carefully chosen, in order to avoid vague generalities. This period, however, gives an unrivalled opportunity for the study of local and manorial government, and although the importance of local history can easily be overstated (for, on the whole, historical perspective must be kept along *national* lines), local feeling is invaluable. It gives flesh and blood to otherwise dry facts of social life, and while no teacher would desire to make his pupils conversant with all the details of local history, it is desirable that all children should know something of the history and growth of their town or village. Local pride cannot be too strongly viewed as the local manifestation of patriotism. Opportunity to serve the country comes to few, but opportunity to serve the locality or the home-town is given to many. Most schools are situated in a district with a "storied past," and it is well worth while to base lessons on social history on actual examples of life in the home-town at various periods, in spite of the difficulty often experienced in the preparation of material.

The following series of lessons prepared for a North Lancashire School, illustrating life in the manor in the fifteenth century, may serve as an example:

1. The manor of Clitheroe in the Middle Ages—the county—the four hundreds—Blackburn—extent of the manor—history—various lords of the manor.
2. Agriculture and the early industries.
3. Trade and the local fairs.

4. How law and order were kept and justice administered, involving a study of the more important of LOCAL COURTS, viz.:

(1) The great court (Sheriff's Turn) once a year—developed into Quarter Sessions.

(2) The court leet of the hundred of Blackburn, having sway over the whole hundred (excepting demesne manors), which was held every three weeks in Clitheroe Castle. But after about 1400 it was only held twice a year, as the less important cases were tried by:

(a) Three weeks' court (Wapentake Court), for recovery of debts under forty shillings, held at Clitheroe Castle and later at Blackburn.

(b) The halmote of the manors of Chatburn, Worston, and Pendleton, usually held on Monday a month after Easter, and at Michaelmas at Clitheroe Castle.

(c) Court of pleas for the borough of Clitheroe (incorp. c.1283), held every three weeks.

(d) Court of Pie-poudré, which settled disputes arising out of the fair. In addition to these, halmotes were held at Colne, Accrington, Haslingden, Tottington, and in the Forest of Bowland; the courts baron of the manor of Slaidburn and the smaller Woodmotes deserve passing reference.

Importance of court roll—evidence of the life of the people—record of bye-laws, etc.

Local Officers: Greave, Constable, Folder, Fence-looker, Ale-taster, etc.

The two chief kinds of court: 1. *Court Baron* and its cases—affairs of manor and the relations of lord and his tenants, arising from their position as land-holders and farmers, *e.g.* quality and welfare of tillage, with enclosures, abuse of pasturage, overcharges, bounds, poaching, etc. Tenants' duties to lord. (As the court sometimes dealt with matters usually associated with courts leet, it is difficult to draw an exact line of demarcation.) 2. *Court Leet*, which dealt with cases of breach of the peace—affrays and bloodsheds, rogues, stocks, "artillery," butts, play and games, "shootings in guns," highways and their repair, rights of way, bridges, felons, profiteers and local trade regulations. (Citizens' duties to community.)

N.B. Privilege of the borough of Clitheroe to hold its own court of pleas to try these cases.

For a teacher, even the mere catalogue of duties, offices, and courts, like the above, is useful; but the matter can be more suitably presented if a small play, based on the charge to a court leet, is written to be acted by the pupils. The following method may serve as a guide to the preparation of a playlet based on a document. Firstly, the class elects its officers:

"Let's suppose we are the discreet and law-abiding men of the manor of Chatburn in the year 1377....We have been cautioned because we have neglected to elect and appoint a reeve...and hasten to do so before the sheriff takes note of it."

Reeve, being elected, recounts his duties (prepared by teacher and read out by *X*): *e.g.* " My duties are many....I watch over the community...in fact it is toilsome to recount all that I have to think of, so that I neglect nothing, not even a mouse-trap or a peg for a hasp.... I am, in truth, a temperate guardian of you men...and must proceed against all evil-doers and present them....I report to the sheriff anything disquieting, etc."

In the same way the *Constable* is elected and recites his duties. Also the minor officers:

Two affeerers :	appointed to settle and moderate fines imposed by the court upon persons "in the mercy of the Court."
Folder :	whose duty it was to look after impounded "strays" in the "folds."
Fence-looker :	keeps watch for broken fences ; also, perhaps, reports damage to bridge (if any) and roads.
Ale-taster :	has general supervision of brewers, bakers, etc. (cf. Inspector of Profiteering).

The above officers having been duly chosen, the class is then in a position to hold a session of the court. A few of the brighter boys can always be found to settle the details and to arrange a rehearsal by the boys who are to be presented. The teacher will find that he has always to modify the enthusiasm of the greave and constable, who evince a desire to arrest the whole country-side for one offence or another ; but after a couple of rehearsals (after school) a lesson is well spent in holding the court.

Procedure.

1. Court assembles.
2. Charges read over by sheriff's officer.
3. Greave presents to sheriff's officer.
4. Constable or folder or ale-taster gives evidence.
5. Accused deny charge or excuse themselves, and call witnesses (again teacher usually has to exercise tact in limiting number of witnesses for the defence).
6. Sentence—fine (fourpence, a pretty stiff fine, being rent of one acre for a year).
7. Affeerer modifies sentence or fine.

A lesson spent in this way really shows the class how their ancestors lived and governed themselves long ago. It also gives them opportunity to co-operate and is itself valuable as a training for citizenship.

The most frequent objection from teachers would be the time this kind of lesson takes to prepare ; but it must be pointed out that the results of one year's "moot" would be very helpful the next, and so it is only the initial preparation that entails time and forethought.

THE CHARGE TO THE JURY

(Based on document *A treatise concerning...a Court Leet Court Baron and Hundred Court etc....*" by J. Wilkinson of Bernards Inne, London, 1638.)

"To the discreet and loyal men...Greeting.
Ye shall take knowledge of, and present to us, all who are meet to be presented, especially those set out below.
First you shall enquire whether there have been any

1. Affrays and Blood-Sheds in the power of the Court, and if any, then those who assaulted must be presented.
2. *Rogues*...said to be by statute...Proctors of Spittlehouses, patent-gatherers, collectors for gaoles, prisons, or hospitals, fencers, bear-wards, common plaires of interludes, minstrels a-wandering abroad, grassemen, saylers, soldiers, schollers, and all other idle persons that goe about begging.
3. *Stockes.* Also for the punishment of the above...you shall enquire if there bee in every tything a paire of stockes according as there

ought to be by statute, or no...if not...then the tything does lose V[li].

4. *Artillery* (after 33 Hen. VIII, c. 9). Everyone is to provide himself with 'a bow and arrowes according to statute. From 17 years to 60 years of age a bow and four arrowes on pain of vj*s*—viiij*d* for every fault. From 7 years to 17 years a bow and 2 arrowes shall be carried.'

5. *Butts.* Ye shall enquire if there is Butts in the borough for the exercise of arching, or the tythings do answer to our sovereign lord for failure.

6. *Plays or Games.* Ye shall enquire if there be any who play with cards, dice, tables, quoits, bowles or such like...for they be un-lawful games...penalty vj*s*—viij*d* for proprietor. And for the purpose of finding and seeking out the above the Constable shall make a monthly search under penalty for not so doing. Unless a man can spend C[li] (pounds) annually then he must not play these games himself, only in his orchard or garden (penalty vi*s*—viij*d*) 'Except in the Christmas time; for then all men may play.'

7. *Shooting in guns.* Ye shall enquire if there be any who do shoot in guns, for they be ill-disposed and dangerous fellows....

8. *Highways kept in order.* Ye shall enquire if the highways are well and truly kept both in order and repair according to direc-tions known to you, or pay the penalty for neglect...for to that end there ought to be two supervisors chosen in every parish by the constables and churchwardens....

9. *Purprestures and Assarts* (18 Ed. II). Ye shall enquire where any wall, hedge, ditch, or house is set abated in the King's highway or any watercourse stopped or turned into the highway to hinder the passage of the King's subjects or in any way annoy them.

10. *Bounds and Marks.* Ye shall enquire if anyone hath moved his neighbour's landmarks...and, if there be any, present them, for it is an evil offence.

11. *Highways or Footsteps.* If anyone has stopped up a lawful passage or stepping-stones, so hindering lawful passage to the Church, mill, or market, present him.

12. *Common Bridges broken or Common Pounds broken.* Ye shall enquire if there be any and take notice of them.

13. *Sleepers by Day and Walkers by Night.* Ye shall enquire if there be any who go about...to steale and purloine other mens goods, conies, fish, hennes...and if so present them, for they are ill members in a commonwealth and deserve punishment.

14. *Eavesdroppers.* Ye shall enquire if there be such as by night stand or by harkening under rails or windows of other men's, to heare what is said in another man's house to the end to set

debate and dissention between neighbours, which is a very evil offence. Therefore, if you know any such, present them.

15. *Forestallers, Regraters, and Ingrossers.* Enquire if there be any ...for they are evil members in a commonwealth. And for a first offence they must serve two months imprisonment without bayle or mainprise, and to forfeit double value of the goods bought or sold. For a second offence they shall have six months imprisonment and forfeit as before. If there be any guilty of a third offence, then shall they be pilloried, and have all their goods confiscate and forfeit to our lord the King, and remain in prison during his royal pleasure.

16. *Butchers.* Ye shall enquire if they sell other than good and wholesome meat for reasonable gains and not at excessive prices.

17. *Shoemakers and Tanners.* Enquire if they make, as they ought, their shoes and bootes of good and well tanned leather...to keep men dry of their legges and feet.

18. *Bakers.* Ye shall enquire if they use only sweet corns and make wholesome bread...also in weight according to the price of wheat in three markets next adjoining, not changing their price...but by sixpence in weight increasing or abating, and if they doe... then they shall be presented and amerced. Also, every baker must set his own proper marke upon every loafe of bread that he maketh and selleth, to the end that if any bread be faultie in weight, it may be then known to whome the fault is.

Also ye shall enquire if the Brewers brew good ale and the Fishers sell good and wholesome fish at a profit not exceeding one penny in twelve of the cost price.

Also shall ye enquire and take notice of false weights and dishonest measures, and if there be any who use such evil measures, them shall ye present.

19. *Drunkards.* Enquire if drunkards are taken and placed for six hours in the stockes according to statute.

20. *Waifs, Strays, and Felons Goods.* Also ye shall enquire if there be any Waifs or cattle stolne and weined out of the possession of him that stole them, and Straies, cattel straid out of their haunt, for they ought to be seized on for the lord's use.

And to conclude if there bee any other thing come to your knowledge meet to be presented...you shall as well enquire thereof and present it with the rest.''

The above charge, based on documents, is a loose adaptation and abbreviation for the purpose of the playlet. It is not complete, but contains most of the matter with which the court—either the three weeks' court or the court of pleas of the borough or the court leet of an outlying manor—would deal.

Its chief function is to show how closely the agricultural and social life of the manor or district was scrutinized, and it throws considerable light on the local government of the time. The court rolls of many districts are extant, and teachers will find most interesting extracts which can be used in this way. They show the other side of the working of the open field system of agriculture, which needed the greatest care and co-operation, and also how heavily the law fell on farmers who were negligent. Thus an extract like the following conveys far more to children of the district than any exposition could do :

Extract from Court Roll of 51 Ed. III, 1377, in the first year of the regality of the County Palatine (19th Sept. 1377):

" Richard, son of William Nowell of Penhulton...for open fences ...iij Gappes in the town of Penhilton is amerced iijᵈ. And, for a barn of the lords dilapidated and thrown down he is amerced iijᵈ... and has to make good the said barn under penalty of xxˢ....And for ij pigs kept continually contrary to the byelaw without rynges and hobbles he is amerced vjᵈ. And for a horse kept contrary to the bye-law, namely, let loose in his neighbours grass, he is amerced ijᵈ."

The class is then able to realize that the open field system not only was a system of agriculture, but, inasmuch as it made close co-operation necessary, it taught their ancestors of the late middle ages *how to govern themselves* and to live peaceably in the country-side—it formed an excellent training-ground for self-government. The good name of the manor or the borough was a matter which touched all, even the humblest of its inhabitants. And these courts, as well as being meetings to settle differences and punish disorders, afforded the country-side or town a means of expressing their wishes. They were like little local parliaments. The vitality of self-government in the shires made possible the early development of central government.

Another useful revision lesson can be devoted to working out a summary in which particular attention is paid to the rights and duties of freemen in the later middle ages, showing :

1. How the country was defended, emphasizing that every freeman was expected to bear arms in defence of the country and giving some description of the stages by which the feudal levy was nationalized and became the nation in arms, as a result of the Oath of Salisbury, "Scutage," the Assize of Arms, and the Statute of Winchester (1285).

2. How order was maintained, emphasizing that every freeman was expected to keep the peace and to assist in suppressing disorder, but that gradually special officers were appointed to help, *e.g.* coroners (special crimes officers), juries of presentment, and conservators of the peace.

3. How disputes were settled, and the share freemen took in the various courts of the boroughs, in the feudal courts, the district (hundred and shire) courts, the royal courts, and the church courts.

4. How laws were made, emphasizing (i) the fact that law-making was rare, as the common law and the customary law usually sufficed ; and (ii) that at first the King made orders and proclamations with or without the consent of the Witan ; later the King legislated "with the assent of the archbishops etc...in parliament assembled " ; but that gradually it was laid down that the King made laws "by and with the consent of Parliament," until by 1485 it was the rule for every new act to have the assent of the Commons, so that after this time the King in Council made Ordinances or Proclamations, but the King in Parliament made Statutes.

It will be necessary to point out that although the

s   7

ordinary freeman may have had little share in the elections
of knights of the shire, or perhaps even of the members for
the cities, nevertheless Parliament did really represent and
speak for England in a remarkably faithful manner.

THIRD YEAR

1. Autumn Term.   Outline of English History, 1485–
   1603 A.D.
2. Spring Term.   Outline of English History, 1603–
   1714 A.D.
3. Summer Term.   Social and Industrial review of the
   period 1485–1714, with special refer-
   ence to later Stuart times, *c.* 1685.

Autumn (1st) Term

Period—*Outline of English History*, 1485–1603

As the syllabus upon which this scheme is based gives so
little time to the political aspect of the period, it is advisable
to leave the consideration of any but the most outstanding
constitutional questions until they arise in Stuart times,
and to regard the Tudor period in its constitutional aspect,
as the prelude to the later struggle between Crown and
Parliament. The civic message of the Tudor period is
patriotism, for never before had England experienced such
a flow of national feeling. The common danger of Spanish
aggression welded England into a nation, a community
proud of their Queen and conscious of their nationality.
The study of the Tudor period ought to leave pupils feeling
a glow of pride in England and a love for the English people.
The war against Spain, the exploits of Hawkins, Drake,
Frobisher, and Sir Richard Grenville, tell their own story
and teach their own lessons; and, happily for teachers, they

are well recorded. The literature of the period, too, reflects its glory; it is the literature of a proud and high-spirited nation—no longer the record of dialect speech, but the refined and melodious song of a people, a race loving England, fearing God, and honouring their sovereign lady, Elizabeth[1].

No period in English history contains so many figures who stride down the centuries and live to-day. Therefore it is wise to let them speak, and to make the most of biography and the least of constitutional issues—small though they were in the period, for it was not pre-eminently an age of constitutional development. Although the seeds of later trouble were sown in this period, and despite the many signs of restlessness in the country and murmured resentment in Parliament against the increasing power of the Crown, yet the popularity and ability of the Tudor rulers, helped by the wave of national spirit consequent on the shock of Spanish aggression, always managed to calm the outburst and postpone the impending but inevitable struggle between Crown and Parliament. Beyond the consideration of the main questions—the increased power and prestige of the Crown and the skill with which the Tudors "managed" Parliament—the teacher will find it advisable to confine himself to the correction of mistaken ideas of the period and to incidental teaching on the constitutional side.

For instance, Henry VII is often dubbed a royal miser; yet his economy and the way he husbanded the resources of the country after the long and costly struggle before his accession deserve credit rather than censure. He was the

[1] It is well to direct pupils' attention to the respect and honour paid to women as a criterion of the manliness and greatness of a people in any age. Even though such a topic can hardly be fully expounded, yet it helps.

leader of the first great anti-waste campaign, and the wisdom of his policy deserves acknowledgment, whatever may have been the motives which inspired it. His policy invites comparison with the work of Walpole after the wars of the eighteenth century and, of course, with the need for economy to-day.

Another incidental point well worth a passing reference is the effect of the invention of gunpowder and the use of fire-arms on the first duty of citizenship—to be prepared to defend the country (*vide* Henry VIII's rules for archery etc.). The passing of the menace of Scottish invasion and the expense and danger of early "musketry practice" caused a neglect of training for national defence, which did not revive until menace from France resulted in the enrolment of "Volunteers."

The Star Chamber and the Court of High Commission are often treated in text-books as if they were from their inception courts which endangered the liberties of citizens, instead of special judicial committees of the Privy Council instituted to deal with special cases for which the common law was felt to be inadequate—hence the idea of most pupils that the Tudors oppressed the people and flouted Parliament; whereas in the reign of Henry VII, at any rate, people were quite content that Parliament should only be summoned seven times in twenty-four years, because the summoning of Parliament invariably meant taxes or "trouble of some sort" for the people in the constituencies, who also had to pay the expenses of their members.

The question of monopolies in Elizabeth's reign gives the teacher an opportunity to point out the growing restiveness against interference with the citizen's liberty to trade; and the way in which Parliament dealt with it shows not only the different temper of the House of Commons but also the different class of man who was now coming forward as member.

Unless full use is made of this incidental teaching, pupils easily get an idea that the liberties of citizens were almost wiped out in Tudor times ; certainly the rights of citizens were somewhat obscured by the conduct of the Crown, but there was no loss of rights nor was the period in any general sense one of oppression or reaction.

THIRD YEAR
Spring (2nd) Term

The Stuart Period—*Outline of political history*

This period covers the age of political strife which moulded our Constitution into its modern form and set the seal on the rights and liberties of English citizens, for after about a century of intermittent struggle between Crown and Parliament our Constitution emerged in its settled form of a "crowned republic." On account of the constitutional issues and the religious under-currents, it is perhaps the most difficult period for pupils and teachers.

It is not pertinent to the present enquiry to trace the course of this struggle, but it is essential to any adequate comprehension of the liberties won for citizens in the period that pupils should start with a clear view of how matters stood on the accession of James I, in order that time may be saved during the outline and that at the end of the period the constitutional progress may be duly appreciated. Therefore it seems advisable that the teacher should give a concise review of the Constitution at the opening of the term, because without this introduction the shifts and expedients to which the Crown resorted, and the protests, petitions, and remonstrances with which Parliament countered them, must be unintelligible and confusing. Pupils can be interested in the struggle, especially if their sporting instincts are aroused; but they must start with a fair view of things, and as the average history text-book glosses over the serious difficulties of the Crown by blaming the personal character and ability of the Stuart Kings, it is necessary at the beginning of the period to describe exactly how matters stood between Crown and Parliament, pointing out that, in the absence of any written Constitution, it was impossible to define the relative rights of King or Parliament with any precision, especially in the matter of revenue and ordinary taxation; and bringing out by striking examples the most material fact that the financial system was entirely unsound[1], as the assessment was antiquated[2], and the cost of government grew heavier each year, while at the same time the purchasing power of money declined. Again, pupils easily overlook the fact that the King was actual head of the executive and personally responsible for national defence, home and foreign affairs, and for any debts incurred by the government; and that even with care and economy he could hardly "make ends meet" or carry on without constant financial help from Parliament in the shape of subsidies, tenths, and fifteenths. It is also necessary to point out that members of Parliament in the Stuart times were drawn from the best families in England; they were men of character and ability, often younger sons of nobility and lords of the manor who had learned the art of ruling and self-government in the counties[3]; in fact, they were the

[1] *E.g.* Elizabeth left a debt of £400,000. At the death of Dorset in 1608 the debt was about £800,000, the annual revenue £427,000, and the expenditure £600,000.

[2] The assessment for subsidies, etc., was still that of 1332.

[3] A list of the names of the members shows this very clearly. Pupils ought to be told who was member for their locality, say, in 1629—very often the family still leads the country-side to-day.

type of men of whom England is proud and to whose descendants we owe much of the successful administration of our Empire—trusty and loyal, yet sturdy and rather stiff-necked men with a high opinion of "the indubitable and inalienable rights of Englishmen[1]."

This gives pupils a fair start, and it will be found that early direction on these lines at the outset of the period is the greatest help and enables pupils to take a keen interest in the constitutional issues of the period. Crown versus Parliament then becomes a game and "fair play" the watch-word. Out of a class of thirty pupils, ten may act as King's men, ten as members of parliament, five as referees, and five as recorders. Then, after a period has been prepared at home, the class becomes a court of record. The teacher calls on the "King," or Laud, or Wentworth to explain his views; next on a parliamentarian to reply; then on the referees to say what seems fair and just; and lastly on the recorders to tell what actually happened and to put it on record. Work of this kind creates its own interest and attention, and the teacher finds his true position as a director and class leader; he becomes rather the stage manager than the leading man, while the class become the company imbued with the spirit of true co-operation. At the end of the period the recorder, whose especial job is writing up the rights and duties of citizens, has a record that really reviews the progress of the period and means something more than "revision" of the ordinary class-room type. Again, such a method enables pupils to take an intelligent interest in the documents with which the period abounds, and, instead of having rather tedious lessons in class based on documents, they are able to read them independently at home. For the documents become "briefs" which must be

---

[1] Of whom Penn is typical.

read in order that pupils may make a fair show when addressing the court of record, and it will be found that pupils make the shrewdest comments on documents as a result of trying to grasp the spirit in which they were drafted[1].

The close of the period forms a good vantage-point from which to review the great advances that had been made towards the complete liberty of the citizen, for by 1714 the rule of law, the sovereignty of Parliament, and the personal liberty and freedom of citizens were practically assured. Except for the removal of the disabilities on Jews, Catholics, and Nonconformists, there has been no great change since then, but only quiet development and widening of the franchise, until modern times (Parliament Act, 1911). If the period has been treated in outline during the term on the lines indicated above, pupils can be set to write out a summary of the rights and protection which citizens had gained, such as below:

1. The personal freedom of the citizen assured by the abolition of arbitrary imprisonment. Stages: (i) Magna Carta; (ii) case of the five knights, 1627 (imprisoned *per speciale mandatum regis*); (iii) the Petition of Right abolished this special Crown order; (iv) the Habeas Corpus Act, 1679.

2. Freedom from arbitrary taxation: *vide* (i) Bates case; (ii) Petition of Right; (iii) John Hampden, 1637; (iv) Bill of Rights, 1689. "Levying...for or to the use of the Crown by pretence of prerogative without grant of Parliament illegal."

3. The right to trade: *vide* struggle against abuse of monopolies, and later (1694) proviso to parliamentary grant to East India Company..."all subjects of England have equal rights to trade to the East Indies unless prohibited by Act of Parliament."

[1] Thus in dealing with the Act of Settlement a pupil comments: "It was a real settlement, not only of the succession and claims of the Crown, but of almost every outstanding constitutional question since Magna Carta...it breathes the spirit of 'England for the English.'...Ministers in future knew where they were...no one could shelter behind the Throne from impeachment, etc...."

4. The right to petition the Crown (*vide* Bill of Rights and Act of Settlement) and to recover land, goods, or money from the Crown by Petition of Right.
5. The right to religious freedom—but not political equality: *vide* disabilities of Jews, Catholics, and Non-conforming bodies.

It will also be seen that great advance had been made in three other directions:

1. Limitations imposed on the Crown (Act of Settlement).
2. The sovereignty of Parliament assured over law-making, over the granting and spending of money (appropriation of supplies), over the army and navy (annual Army Act, etc.) and in a measure over the judges (*vide* method of appointment and dismissal). In fact, Parliament supreme over all rivals—the King or either House of Parliament.
3. The freedom of the press. Stages: (i) in the nature of a royal monopoly; (ii) under censorship of Star Chamber; (iii) under power of Parliament by annual or periodic licensing acts; (iv) 1695, refusal to pass annual act and as a result the press just stumbled into freedom and became an indirect limitation on the power of Parliament itself by focussing public opinion on its deliberations.

THIRD YEAR

SUMMER (3RD) TERM

SOCIAL HISTORY OF ENGLAND IN THE SIXTEENTH AND SEVENTEENTH CENTURIES

The chief aim of this term's work is to give pupils some idea of the people, their work and play, in Tudor and Stuart times, and therefore no special lessons dealing with the rights and duties of citizens are necessary, because the course shows the people in their every-day life fulfilling their duties. Back-ground and local colour are the main essentials; and there is such a bewildering mass of material that selection becomes most difficult and would be well-nigh impossible if it were not that the native interests of pupils form such a helpful guide and indicate a study of costume, folk gentle and simple, their houses, furniture, and gardens, work, play and games, ships and sailors, schools and scholars, etc. In twenty periods of school-work supplemented by twenty periods of preparation it is only possible to give a series of glimpses or peeps into the life of the people, but they can be vivid and exact[1].

With so crowded a term, it is evident that any consideration of matters relating to government and citizenship must be incidental and in the nature of side-talks. Opportunity for these occurs in plenty—thus, for instance, a consideration of the number of sturdy beggars and the Poor Law of 1601 gives a starting-point for one of the themes which ought to receive attention throughout the whole subsequent course of study. Pupils can be encouraged to open a sort of folio in their note-books in which they will enter the chief acts designed to ameliorate the lot of the poor—an account which would look back to the work of the monasteries and mediaeval charities and forward to the Poor Laws of the nineteenth century, the Old Age Pension Act, and the Report of the Poor Law Commission of 1911; for the care of the poor, the aged, and the infirm is a factor well worthy of the attentions of citizens to be.

Again, arising out of the administration of the Poor Law or the work of the country gentleman, attention must be directed to the work and importance of the Justices of the Peace. Pupils will notice the decay of the shire and hundred courts and also of the smaller manor courts, once so important in local government; and that the Sheriffs, shorn even of their military duties by the Lords Lieutenant, had gradually sunk into the position of ornamental functionaries. The Justices of the Peace meeting in the Quarter Sessions

[1] Naturally the teacher will make the greatest possible use of pictures and of local records, illustrations, and monuments.

had become the ruling spirits in the counties, not only dispensing justice in the petty courts, but deciding matters of county administration and government—fixing wages, assessing levies for the hated poor rate, drawing up rules for the suppression of disorder and for the repair of the roads, and many other lesser duties. There are many excellent descriptions of them and their work extant, and pupils will see that they were typically English, unpaid and with no special qualifications, but that they managed to carry on the local administration and justice with sturdy common-sense, and, under the watchful eye of Secretaries of State like Burleigh, with considerable efficiency. The part they played in the history of the Stuart period can scarcely be over-estimated and pupils cannot get any insight into the social life of the period unless this is adequately presented.

During this term a lesson might be set aside for a description of the rise and state of any ancient local industry. For instance, at Sheffield the pupils in secondary schools who will be the leading citizens when they reach manhood ought not to leave school without some knowledge of the history of the great cutlery industry for which their city is famous. It will certainly stimulate pride in their city, and though the Sheffield of James I's time, as described by Macaulay, was not a pleasant place, it invites comparison with Sheffield to-day.

Again, if any locality has legal or constitutional features of local interest, such as the "Gibbet Law" at Halifax, or the ancient privilege of the Soke of Peterborough to try criminals who otherwise would have been dealt with at the Sessions or Assizes, it is desirable that these features should find some place, however modest, in the school syllabus.

It may be urged against this that these matters are not national, that they belong to the realm of antiquaries rather than to history, and are out of place in schools because they foster a narrow and parochial spirit and tend to give pupils an exaggerated idea of the importance of their home-town or city. But, against this, it must be remembered that, with the increasing facilities for travel and for wide reading, and particularly with the nationalizing influence of the press, it is becoming more and more necessary to foster this local patriotism, which is rather in danger of decaying than of growing so strong that it leads to narrowness and local selfishness. And this is especially so to-day, when the dead hand of bureaucracy is so menacing; therefore if the schools can help local spirit by retelling the storied past, it is worth every effort to do so.

The rise of the great mercantile corporations, such as the East India Company, consequent on the great expansion of trade, affords a convenient land-mark from which to review the rise of the capitalist system in the realm of trade. The beginning of the rise of large-scale production is obscure and beyond the scope of school study; but the early workings of the system enable the teacher to present to pupils a clearer view of its merits and demerits than is possible at a later period. Beginning with the mediaeval merchants, such as Whittington or de la Pole, who were wealthy enough to equip vessels and send out little argosies of their own, it is easy to review the change to ventures where several people subscribed money to fit out ships and finance a voyage. Pupils can see how private enterprise of this sort flourished in the sixteenth and seventeenth centuries—the Cabots and Hawkins are outstanding examples—and that the impulse was quickened by the knowledge of the inadequate protection which Spain gave to her gold convoys and the ease with which they were to be plundered. But since patriotic plunder soon gave way to trade, in the absence of any policing of the seas this trade had to be regulated, for all sorts of complications would continually arise out of the quarrels of English and foreign venturers; therefore unregulated trade (which was tried for a time under the Commonwealth) gradually gave way to regulated trade under chartered companies. Private traders often did not return, because other nations (chiefly the Dutch) had formed companies, and, unless small fleets went out together adequately equipped and protected, there was not much hope of success. The advantages of collective enterprise were obvious; the company soon had a capital and shareholders—it was a corporation and responsible to the State, and it continued to trade until it failed or its charter was taken away. From time to time a dividend was paid by the company to its shareholders in proportion to the amount they had subscribed or invested; but the main portion of the original capital was still vested in the company, and this was a distinct advance on the older system of dividing everything on the conclusion of the venture.

A consideration of the genesis of capitalism and large-scale production leads to other aspects of the financial system of the sixteenth and seventeenth centuries; for the beginnings of country banks, the earlier activity of the goldsmiths, the safe deposit in the Tower, the seizure of the deposits by Charles I, and the "failure" of Charles II are all of great interest. The parliamentary control over coinage and revenue which followed the revolution of 1688 paved the way for borrowing on the security of the State in times of emergency from those who had savings. This marked the beginning of national credit as opposed to royal credit, and it is easy to demonstrate how the wealth of the nation was increased by the operation of this credit and by the beginnings of scientific finance. Pupils can see how helpful it was to merchants to be able to borrow money to further and increase their business at a fairly fixed and known rate of interest, so that enterprising ventures were no longer at the mercy of Shylocks and unscrupulous usurers; they realize that the year 1694 is famous for the foundation of the Bank of England. They can see how the number of citizen creditors tended to avert revolution and give stability to ordered government. Many pupils in schools to-day have helped the nation by their thrift and foresight in buying War Saving Certificates, and they will be found keenly interested in what seems rather a dry subject if it is only suitably presented. Short and lively talks of this nature help to make school history touch the world of to-day, and ultimately lead pupils to realize that "the State is ourselves."

FOURTH YEAR

1. AUTUMN TERM. 1714–1815.
2. SPRING TERM. 1815–1918.
3. SUMMER TERM. Constitutional, social, and industrial review of the Nineteenth Century, and the study of particular topics.

AUTUMN (1ST) TERM

PERIOD—1714–1815

It is fortunate that the period covered by the first term's work was one of constitutional adjustment and settlement rather than change; it therefore does not call for more than incidental teaching from the point of civic instruction. The period includes the long struggle with France in India and

America, the American War of Independence, the French
Revolution, and the war against Napoleon on the political
side; and on the social and economic side, the beginnings
of the vast changes consequent on the Industrial Revolution.
With so wide a survey it is evident that for school purposes
the century must be treated in broad outline.

In the first half of the eighteenth century, the quiet development of Cabinet government under Walpole and the
withdrawal of the King from the council of ministers is
remarkable. There was also growing up the idea of loyalty
to the head of the Cabinet, which Walpole insisted on and
which came to be regarded as an unwritten rule after his
long term of office. The position of Prime Minister as the
responsible head of the ministry, possessing the chief weight
in the council and the principal place in the confidence of
the King, must be noted, and with it the rise of ministerial
unity, so that if a minister disagreed with the premier's
policy, he was expected to resign; for by the middle of the
century the premier's policy had become the policy of the
government, for which the Cabinet as a whole were responsible. This was a quiet development and slow-growing, but
it is important because it shows the transition to present-
day policy. During the term some consideration ought to
be given to the party system, so as to bring out what the
political life of England owed to its development, *e.g.*
constitutional stability and the maintenance of the respect
due to the Crown, etc.

The question of parliamentary corruption under Walpole's
ministry (and later as used by the King in his attempts to
influence Parliament) needs attention; and the importance
of the "place clause" in the Act of Settlement and the
Place Act in 1708 needs pointing out, because these Acts,
together with the long government of Walpole and the

withdrawal of the King from the Cabinet, all tended to increase the power of Parliament, which became no longer a deliberating assembly, or an assembly to be consulted by the government, but a government-making body. By the time that George III attempted to increase the power of the Crown this was a recognized political fact, and therefore the Crown, in order to control the government, had to gain control of a majority in Parliament. Hence the corruption and abuse of the Royal patronage in order to secure a large number of " King's Friends " in the House.

The struggle which centred in the unworthy and dissolute Mr Alderman Wilkes calls for attention, because it marks a further stage in the advance towards complete liberty of the individual and it shows Parliament enforcing its privileges against its own unruly members by an illegal device —the General Warrant; but it does not seem necessary to spend much time on this struggle, although the feeling shown in the country at the time is important, as it shows the need for Parliamentary reform, which was soon to be the most important point in home policy.

We have said that the eighteenth century was not an age of constitutional change; but the last half of the century was a great age of political thought and of parliamentary oratory. The former aspect is beyond the scope of school study, but the latter is well within it; and no course of school history ought to be complete unless the pupils have had opportunity to read and study the greater speeches of Edmund Burke and of Pitt, Earl of Chatham. These speeches, particularly Burke's speeches on American Taxation (April 19th, 1774) and on "Conciliation with the Colonies" (March 22nd, 1775) and Chatham's speeches on America, are classics, and cannot fail to impress students. Burke's letter to the Sheriffs of Bristol, especially the following passage, ought to be as well-known by English pupils as Lincoln's address at Gettysburg is known by American pupils.

Certainly, Gentlemen, it ought to be the happiness of a representative to live in the strictest union with his constituents. Their wishes ought to have great weight with him. ... It is his duty to sacrifice his repose, pleasure, satisfaction to theirs, and above all to prefer their interests to his own. But his unbiassed opinion, his mature judgement, his enlightened conscience he ought not to sacrifice to any man or to any set of men living. Your representative owes you not only his industry but his judgement, and he betrays you instead of serving you, if he sacrifices it to your opinion.

Indeed, all pupils in the senior forms should be encouraged to read the Life of Burke by Lord Morley as home reading —it is a splendid introduction to political thought; Burke's broad mind, his reasonableness, judgment, and lucidity fill one with admiration and leave an impression which is abiding. "Show the thing you contend for to be reasonable, common sense, and useful, and I am content" (American Taxation). "I do not know the method of drawing up an indictment against a whole people." "Nobody shall persuade me, when whole people are concerned, that acts of lenity are not means of conciliation." Quotations like these ought to be learnt by heart, because in after-life they have a way of recalling themselves and tend to exert a steadying influence; and if there was ever a need for quiet and sober judgment in the educated classes, it is at the present time and during the next few years. It is better to teach the truths so well expressed by Burke than to neglect them altogether, because there is not time for an adequate study of the life of Burke in school hours.

The Declaration of the Rights of Man (1789) and the Declaration of American Independence (1776) ought to be read and studied by pupils during their course, because they are land-marks in the progress towards democracy. It will

s   8

be found extremely difficult—apart from the lack of time
—to set exercises on these documents, and they are probably
best read over in class and discussed freely in the "gather
round and let's have a look at this" spirit. Many teachers
who are enthusiastic believers in the use of "sources" and
documents sometimes fall into the error of setting exercises
on all documents. This is a dangerous practice. The
documents themselves may be quite suitable for use as illustration, or for conveying historical knowledge and evidence,
although exercises set on them, however ingeniously con-
trived, may be quite unsuitable. Further, the practice tends
to create a dislike of documents in the minds of pupils.

FOURTH YEAR
Spring (2nd) Term

Period—*The Nineteenth Century* (1815–1918)

In a term of twenty periods supplemented by twenty
lessons of preparation it is evident that the century can
only be treated in outline, and that the teacher must rely
on the study of special topics in the next term to amplify and
give life to the outline. This is a useful allocation, because the
study of the special topics cannot be really fruitful unless
the whole period has previously been covered. As the main
aim of this term must be to cover the whole period and give
it perspective, no special lessons such as have been a feature
of the previous years, illustrating the rights and duties of
citizens and the development of our Constitution, are called
for, especially as the outline of the citizen's share in the four
main functions of government—defence, order, justice, and
law-making—no longer suffice, since a higher and nobler
conception of citizenship gradually prevailed. At the
opening of the period liberty was assured, and early in the

century political equality was realized, but fraternity was sadly lacking. As the century unfolds itself, pupils must be led to see that the community again begins to be regarded as a family, and the government, which in the earlier and most distressful years of the century acted like a stern and repressive father, gradually becomes more like a watchful and kindly mother, and that this conception was reflected in the conception of citizenship. The possession of the vote ceased to be a worthy criterion, giving place to the nobler conception of social service or applied fraternity; the great citizens invariably were the great humanitarians.

Teachers will admit that this is a most difficult period for school study; the heroic figures have left the stage, and boys of fifteen or sixteen are not easily interested in the bald outline of a rather drab age, such as the first half of the century. Happily, adolescence brings many gifts, and not the least of these is that the boy, having found his own soul, begins vaguely to appreciate the inestimable value of other human souls, and so the wave of humanitarianism which cleansed and purified the stagnant waters of the century awakes some response in his heart and mind. If from the beginning the period is so presented as to show man rising phoenix-like from the drabness and squalor in which the hectic flush of the Industrial Revolution and the fevered rush of the few to enrich themselves had left him, pupils are invariably interested. In short, fraternity must be the key-note of the presentation and study, for this is the summation of civic teaching.

At the beginning of the term some direction must be given by the teacher, because the politics of the nineteenth century must remain vague and unconvincing unless pupils realize the state of England in the years 1815–20. The teacher is well advised to describe and to illustrate by striking examples and statistics the state of the roads, the general lack of news, the absence of popular education, the state of local government and the share taken by the parson and the squire in the parishes, the boroughs, their government and courts, the parliamentary boroughs, the county franchises, and the outstanding anomalies of the electoral system. Some introduction of this kind is all the more necessary as many text-books afford pupils no adequate description of these factors. In all probability some direction will also be necessary to introduce the social and economic aspects of the century, for the story of the misery and poverty of the working classes in the earlier part of the century seems unbelievable, though it is essential to any adequate estimate of the progress that has been made. Although this introduction is necessary for effective study, it must be concise and in the nature of "what to look out for" rather than full or erudite, showing the close connection between the eighteenth and nineteenth centuries, and the changes due to the stimulus of new ideas and conceptions of human and civic relationships which affected the whole trend of legislation. It must show that the changes in the system of industry and the consequent massing of great numbers of people in towns brought evils, but at the same time, by aggravating and exposing them, paved the way to the reform of Parliament and of local government. Early in the term the attention of pupils may well be directed to two other factors—the settlement and expansion of the Empire, and the growth of a sense of right among nations. In dealing with the growth of the Empire, many of the details of acquisition and conquest may well give place to make time for some outline of how it is governed to-day, showing the spread of British ideals of citizenship and self-government. Generally speaking, the growth of a sense of right among nations and its expression in International Law is too difficult a subject for school study, but in the course of their fourth year pupils can be directed to notice that this sense of right was gradually growing, and that home opinion and policy were becoming more and more sensitive to Western European thought and action and to the influence of the liberal and reforming spirit abroad. Pupils will see that England, imbued with a proud and conscious spirit of nationality, is not, and cannot be, insensible to the sufferings and the aspirations of other nations; and also, that out of the spirit of nationality in its fulness will come that international sense of right and justice and that desire for international peace and friendship which is the hope of the world[1]. In short, the "applied fraternity," or humanitarianism, which in the nineteenth century was largely national, must become more and more international in the future, because this alone will make the twentieth century the age of fulfilment, even as the nineteenth century was the age of hope.

If these introductory lectures and "directions" occupy five periods of school study, fifteen remain in which to study the century in outline, and, supplemented by an equal number of periods of preparation, this ought to allow sufficient time for an outline which will be more than a mere frame-work. During the term pupils can be encouraged to open folios in their note-books similar to the one already indicated for the Poor Laws, in which to enter the benefits citizens gained during the century under headings such as: justice (the reform of the penal code, right of appeal etc.),

[1] Pupils may be led to realize that nations will never be too poor or too proud to fight each other, but they may become too sensible. War will never be stopped by the fear of its consequences, but only by the growth of a common conscience and "the enthusiastic love of the general good."

religious equality, freedom of thought, education and the care of children, freedom of association, etc.; for, if this is done, the work in the third term on special topics becomes revision in its best sense, the study of the nineteenth century fulfils its true function in preparing pupils for an understanding of social and political life to-day, and the need for a text-book of civics recedes as the story of the century is unfolded.

FOURTH YEAR
SUMMER (3RD) TERM

THE STUDY OF SPECIAL TOPICS

If the scheme has been followed, the pupils have covered the history of England and the Empire in outline, and the last term is left free for the study of special topics. The full development of the last century has been so many-sided that, unless some definite aim guides the selection, the work becomes merely sporadic revision. Let us be guided in our selection by the usefulness of the topics to pupils as citizens to be.

This gives us a worthy criterion, but there is a further test. Can the lessons be presented in such a way as to train the pupil's observation, critical faculty, and judgment? This, of course, is not, and cannot be, an absolute test, owing to the many limitations which surround us as teachers, but it is very important as the most desirable method of presentation.

The caveats relative to the teaching of the most recent periods of history have been so aptly expressed by Dr Keatinge in his *Studies in the Teaching of History* and also in the chapter dealing with "Politics as a School Subject" in *Studies in Education* (A. & C. Black) that we cannot do better than quote from them.

Firstly, in dealing with the appeal made to youthful minds, he says "The young can be reached only by judicious personal allusion, social theory must arise out of social fact, and the fact must be a fact of daily life that they can understand" (see *Studies in Education*, Chapter IX).

Secondly, when indicating the need for a rigorous method of history teaching, he points out that "the normal healthy adolescent mind readily adopts an attitude of contrariance when attempts are made to introduce to it ideas which embody notions of morality or of conduct. The more directly these moral ideas are introduced the stronger tends to be the reaction against them, unless the person or the situation which introduces them is sufficiently masterful or impressive to inhibit this contrariance by introducing a strong emotional tone. Much teaching of this kind, while in a certain sense it might be effective, would not in the long run make for the moral or intellectual welfare of the pupil."

It is very necessary to bear these cautions in mind during the teaching of the most recent periods, especially as the economic aspects of history and their interpretations cause such divergence of opinion. The method of teaching by documents helps a teacher who has decided political views to avoid showing them during his teaching, because, as far as possible, he can leave his pupils to form their own conclusions from the documents, regarding the selection and grouping of suitable documents and illustrations and the correction of the conclusions drawn by the pupils as his chief share of the work. But, even so, in the correction of the pupils' wrong ideas and conclusions the political predilections of the teacher must peep out, no matter how carefully he may hide them. He may be unable to avoid stating his personal opinions, but, provided that he states the case for the opposing side equally clearly and emphatically and takes care to label his opinions as *his* opinions, the danger of partiality is greatly lessened. Teachers have every right to decided political views and to a free field for political activity in common with all other citizens, but in school, the stronger a man's opinions may be, the less he ought to speak of them, and the greater care he must take to avoid partiality in exposition, illustration, or the interpretation of historical development.

While a term's work spent almost entirely on the study of documents and sources relevant to the chosen topics seems the best course, yet the difficulties and the time taken up in gathering together a suitable body of documents and illustrations render it almost impossible at first. The work of collection must go steadily forward, but meanwhile the teacher has to depend very largely on his powers of clear and sustained exposition. If suitable text-books are available, the pupil may be set to work out the themes; but, as a text-book gives the conclusions of others, and as modern text-books are not quite free from bias, this is not so desirable as work from sources, backed, if necessary, by full chronological summaries or epitomes (without comments, merely stating facts).

Keeping the above aims and cautions in mind, we have a three-fold task: firstly, we must make a selection of suitable topics; secondly, we must aim at gathering together material to illustrate those topics; thirdly, we must decide what is the most effective method of teaching or presenting the subjects.

Let us consider them in order:

I. **Choice of topics.** The selection of topics useful to our pupils as future citizens, helping them to understand the problem of to-day, is affected very largely by the practicability of getting together a suitable text and illustrations;

but although it may not be possible to obtain such matter at first, yet it is well to set down the topics which are most worthy of a place, leaving for the moment the question of the accessibility of documentary and other illustration.

The topics set out below represent a body of knowledge which would afford a young citizen some guidance on the problems which confront the community to-day, and also throw some light on the recent development of the machinery of government and the making of modern England.

1. The development of democratic government and the consequent changes in:

(i) The Defence of the Country.
  The Army—Navy—Crimea—Reform—Volunteers—Militia—Territorials—"Kitchener's Army"—Conscription—The Citizen Army—Demobilization—Obligations.

(ii) The Maintenance of Order.
  Review in earlier times—Obligations on all within the law—Lawlessness in eighteenth century—Peel's Act, 1828—Municipal Police, 1835—County Police—Watch Committees—Intelligence Branch—Bow Street Runners—Detective Force—Rights and Duties of all Citizens.

(iii) The Administration of Justice.
  Law Courts: Imperial and Local—The Bar and Solicitors—The confusion and delay resulting in the High Court of Judicature Act, 1873—Courts of Appeal : (*a*) Criminal, (*b*) Civil, (*c*) Ecclesiastical and Colonial.

(iv) The Making of Laws.
  (*a*) Imperial: the extension of franchise—very little change in parliamentary procedure—freedom of speech—reporting—importance of publication of parliamentary debates and division lists—the Cabinet—chief officers.
  (*b*) Local: Municipal Reform—Bye-laws.

2. The efforts of the working classes to improve their lot:

(i) Trades Unions. (ii) Friendly Societies. (iii) The Co-operative movement.

3. The effects of the introduction of machinery and mass production:

(i) National production. (ii) The means of communication. (iii) The grouping and social life of the people.

4. The improvement in national health.

5. The improvement in housing.

6. The provision for the poor, the aged, and infirm.

7. The rise of banking.

8. The growth of newspapers, abolition of "taxes on knowledge," and the power of the Press.

9. The revival of local government.

10. The progress of science and invention, in relation to :

(i) Steam. (ii) Electricity. (iii) Aviation. (iv) Oil-fuel engines.

11. Progress in education, with special reference to the opportunities for the average citizen and the foundation of a national system of education.

While these topics cannot be held to cover the many-sided activity of the nineteenth century, they will be useful to the pupils as future citizens. It may be objected that only the first topic has any direct bearing on citizenship, and this is true if the subject is regarded in its narrower sense; but our aim is to give the pupil an insight into the history of the century which will enable him to become an intelligent and useful citizen.

Naturally, in so short a period, he cannot get more than an insight into these questions, but if these history lessons stimulate his curiosity and give direction to his adult reading, then a great advance has been made on present-day conditions. The seed sown may bear fruit and help to awaken that habit of thinking *for* others and *of* others which is essential for citizenship.

In the last term of school life it is not practicable for each pupil or pair of pupils to have time for study of all the topics, under existing arrangements; but it is most helpful if they can study one each week—that means two lessons and two periods of preparation, with perhaps an extra period given to the first topic, which all should study.

The class-room or lecture-room is quite unsuited to the work in these final stages, as it is necessary that pupils should have complete freedom to move about and get necessary material from books. As a rule, a fourth or fifth form is not so large as the lower forms, and pupils can conveniently be seated in the school library. For the history teacher the school library is the school laboratory, and this last year's work must be regarded as laboratory or experimental work. It is a testing time. The educational value of teaching pupils to use books intelligently and familiarly, proving in practice that books really are "treasure-houses of knowledge," needs no emphasis.

It will be found most helpful to allow pupils to work in pairs, and as far as possible each pair should be set to work on different topics. At first, pupils are slow in "handling" and collecting material, and the use of books—that is, books of reference, as apart from text-books—seems strange to them. But they soon acquire considerable speed and facility; and although at first the teacher may have to give more help and direction than he may think is desirable, the pupils soon "carry on" for themselves. The feeling of "not knowing where to begin" is very much lessened by the system of working in pairs. The objection that two "slackers" working together do less work than the same boys working independently has weight, but this can be avoided or corrected by the master. As a rule, if a boy is not doing his share, his partner is prompt to tell him so, and once the pair look on their work as "our show," then they put forth their best efforts. Again, in answering the questions set on the documents the differences of opinion that arise between the two are most useful. Even in reading through a document pupils will differ as to the meaning of a passage or the reliability of evidence, and this is all to the good[1].

It is desirable that some pupils should be encouraged to choose a subject on which to give a short lecture to the class. This helps to give them confidence in speaking, clarifies their ideas, and also tends to make them less ruthless in their judgments and less downright in their interpretation of material. The young lecturer knows quite well that he will be rigorously taken to task by his class-mates for sweeping statements or bias, and the sobering effect of the method is soon felt. The pupil may require more time for his particular topic than for others, but it will be found that, as pupils choose a subject in which they are keenly interested, most of the extra work required is done in the pupils' spare time.

II. **The collection of material.** In his wider leisure reading the teacher will always be on the look-out for matter which illustrates the topics he considers most advisable for his pupils to study. The teacher of history, more than any other teacher, needs a book in which he can enter extracts or references, so that, on consulting his note-book, he knows at once where to find the extract he considered suitable and the topic which it illustrated. It is useful to have this book indexed either for topics or alphabetically.

If any useful book is not already in the school library and is too expensive to be purchased, it is worth while to have the extract typed or written out. As a rule, however, it will be found that these journals and other similar documents have been well searched, and probably the passage has already been included in some edition of contemporary documents or sources. Although it is hardly

[1] It would be worth while to appoint a commission of five or seven pupils to make a report on a topic—and hope for a minority report.

possible to have more than one set of documents in use for class work, yet an effort should be made to include as many books of "sources" as possible in the school library. For instance, there is an admirable selection grouped under topics published by the Oxford Press and edited by Mr Turrill, which presents many documents not included in the better-known collection of Keatinge and Frazer. And so it is with other works of the same class; as far as possible, they should all be in the school library and the documents contained in them gradually entered in a register and index of sources and illustrations[1]. To give any directions as to the compilation of the index book, beyond advising a grouping under topics and suggesting a column for short *précis*—which need only be two or three words denoting the particular phase of the topic upon which the extract has bearing— seems quite unnecessary, because each specialist thinks his own system best, and for him it is best, because he has to use it. The value of such a record for the final work in the upper forms can hardly be over-stated. It takes time to compile—perhaps two or three years before it is satisfactory, but the time saved later on, and the advantages gained, far outweigh the trouble expended. Once the idea of the record is explained, the senior pupils are keen to add a valuable extract or illustration, and the pupils also gain, in so far as

---

[1] Most secondary schools have commercial sides and classes which might usefully practise their typing in reproducing useful matter like this; or even as an imposition it might be useful to insist on a pupil copying out useful material instead of writing lines. (This is the least desirable method of augmenting the collection.) The advantages of loose-leaf books for the index book and also for any register of illustrative documents cannot be overlooked; also for any large "topic-book" or "source-book" the same holds good. Teachers can make these large loose-leaf scrap-books themselves; they are cheaper, more easily handled, can have leaves added or taken out, etc. In short, what the loose-leaf ledger has done in economizing time in business houses cannot be overlooked in schools.

they set to work on their topic in a methodical way, learning the use of indexes and the value of books.

III. **The teacher's method.** If the pupils have had some training in the use of books, and particularly larger books of reference, little introduction is necessary, in which case the teacher would withdraw himself as much as possible and only help a pair when they had exhausted their own efforts to solve a question or to unearth relevant material. Although he may know quite well what they are seeking, he would, as far as possible, indicate where it is to be found rather than supply the information off-hand.

At first, owing to lack of material and experience of this kind of work, the teacher may have to draw out a rough programme of work for each pair, but later, when the material has been gathered and roughly indexed, it is only necessary for him to name the topic and to indicate the sources and the questions.

There are many collections of illustrations which already are most useful, such as Barnard's *Companion to English History in the Middle Ages* (Oxford Press), to which the student can be referred, but in England there is no collection of illustrated matter comparable to the French *Album Historique* by Lavisse. Teachers will find that this work, on the pictorial side, is a good example of the sort of books from which their source-books can be compiled, and reference to chap. XV ("Les Armes françaises au XIX Siècle") will show the kind of illustrations well worth recording. In dealing with the topic of education in the nineteenth century the illustrations in Tome 4, p. 255 ("L'Enseignement primaire") of the *Album Historique* may be compared with the illustrations given in Birchenough's *History of Elementary Education* (University Tutorial Press).

SPECIAL TOPICS

Taking the first topic, treating the functions of Government, with special reference to the rights and duties of citizens in the nineteenth century, as an example, let us see how the collection of material would progress.

(i) *The Defence of the Country.*

At first the pupils would not have the advantage of a record-book containing a collection of relevant material and illustration, and they would have to be directed to make a summary such as the one below. Most of this could be got from any good history note-book, such as Rolleston's *English History Note Book* (Davis and Houghton), filled in by reference to *The British Army* by the Hon. J. W. Fortescue (Macmillan), while a good sketch of the whole subject is given in Chapter XIX of *The Rights and Duties of the English Citizen* by H. E. Malden (Macmillan).

The standing army. Lack of Crown forces in Tudor times (recall Pilgrimage of Grace and other insurrections)—the Civil Wars —Cromwell's New Model—the Restoration—idea of standing army slowly accepted—James II's abuse of army—attempt to make army a means of oppression—the Glorious Revolution—first Mutiny Act, 1689, a national safeguard—the Household Cavalry—the Foot Guards, etc.

The militia (cf. Fyrd). The real basis of national defence for many centuries—acts enforcing equipment and training (see Assize of Arms, etc.)—the real church parades (after church, weapon-showing).

1747. Reorganization of Militia after failure of '45—Militia-men *chosen by lot*, implying that every able-bodied man was under obligation to serve.
Enrolment of Highland Regiments.

1803. The Volunteers (additional to the Militia), but *not* taking away obligation of all citizens to serve.

1808. The Militia Act.

1815. Volunteers disbanded, except Cavalry and Yeomanry.

1847. Short Service Act—shortened period of enlistment.

1852. Militia again reorganised on basis of voluntary enlistment. The obligation of each citizen to be trained and equipped for defence of the country obscured by this act.

1854. The office of Secretary of State for War separated from that of the Colonial Secretary (cf. Secretary of State for War and Air, 1921).

1858. Institution of Victoria Cross.

1859. Volunteer Movement—great wave of patriotism.

1863. Volunteer Act.

1867. Reserve Force Act, founding the Militia Reserve, a body of troops who in case of war become regular soldiers.

1870. War Office Act. The Commander-in-Chief becomes the chief officer of army *under* the Secretary of State.

1871. Abolition of the purchase of Commissions. All forces under command of Crown (in effect, under Secretary of State for War).

1879. Army Discipline Act; also short act passed each year sanctioning the rules of the army—the *King's Regulations.*

1881. Abolition of flogging in the Army.

1907. Reforms at War Office under Lord Haldane.
Creation of the Territorial Force: Artillery—Yeomanry—Cavalry—Infantry—Officers' Training Corps.

1914. The Great War—the "Old Contemptibles" (cf. Bismarck's gibe on "Police")—the rise of a citizen army—work of Lord Kitchener—voluntary system abandoned—"Derby scheme"—obligation of all to serve gradually acknowledged.

1917–18. Conscription Act.

1918. Armistice.

1918–20. Demobilization—Ministry of Pensions—efforts to recompense those who have suffered and the bereaved.

1920. Unveiling of the Cenotaph—burial of Unknown Warrior in Westminster Abbey.

It is not to be expected that pupils will be able to make out a summary quite as full as this at first, and though at the inception of the scheme their attempts may be much more "sketchy" than the above, they gain a great deal in "looking up" the matter. Later on, the best summary can be entered in the opening pages of the record-book dealing with the topic of national defence. A convenient form is to make a line of time and have a fairly comprehensive summary of events on one page, and on the opposite page give references where illustrations and explanatory material can be found, in this way:

Nineteenth century	Documents and Illustrations	See page
1800		
.		
.	Pictures of uniforms	25
. Volunteers enrolled ...	Martello towers etc.	26
.	Account of Mr Pitt in camp as Colonel of Cinque Port	
*	Volunteers	28
.		
.		
.		
. Militia Act	Account of Mustering	30
1810		
.		
.		
.		

The books can be made of plain paper, which will take
ink; it is very desirable to have them large—about eleven
by fourteen inches is a convenient size—and loose leaves
are a necessity. Brown paper boards made in the art room,
with suitably designed stencils, make effective bindings.
Once the idea of the record-book is explained to the pupils,
they take the greatest interest in finding suitable illustrations. All boys love collecting, and the teacher is soon
provided with illustrations and useful matter. The difficulty
is not to get material, but to select what is most useful for
school purposes. In a few years the school has records of
the greatest interest. Teachers can appoint their senior
pupils to be "Keepers of the Records," each senior pupil
being responsible for a record-book during his last year. A
list of the keepers soon relieves the master from being
attacked at inconvenient times by enthusiastic collectors,
because the boys soon get to know who is in charge of the
record for which they have likely material.

s   9

It may be urged that, in order to carry out this scheme, the history master would need thirty hours in a day, and perhaps it appears to readers that the scheme is more desirable than practicable; but when it has been working a week or two it will be found that ten minutes once a week, or even a fortnight, is all that is required for a meeting of the record-keepers and the history master, because in many cases only a reference may be necessary.

The teacher's attitude in looking over the work done by the pupils will naturally be more suggestive than corrective, as the main object is to stimulate curiosity. Questions like the following occur to one:

Has the Army ever shown that it was affected by national popular feeling in any time of crisis?

In view of the absence of Crown forces in Tudor times, do you think it right to speak of the "Tudor despotism"?

Can you see any resemblance between the house-carls of Saxon and Danish times and the Household Cavalry of to-day?

When did the citizen's obligation of military service become obscured?

When was the County Militia called out for the last time in history to ward off an enemy landing?

Have you read *A Private of the Buffs*, or how Grenville fought in "The Revenge," or how Jack Cornwell won the V.C., or how we landed at Gallipoli, or Kipling's *Recessional*.

Do you remember what Pericles said in consoling the relatives of the heroes who fell in the Peloponnesian War?

In this way boys see for themselves that the spirit is still the same, and it wins every time in every age, whether shown in a local cricket match or a great war. The actual examples of grit and bravery make their own appeal.

(ii) *The Maintenance of Law and Order.*

What has been done on the subject of national defence forms a guide to the treatment of the maintenance of order. But it is much more difficult to trace the rise of our police forces than that of the armed forces. The rights and duties of the citizen (law-abiding citizen) are not so clear, and the reading involved is more general. Through all our history —since the tythings sought to enforce collective responsibility for policing a district—all men within the law have been bound not only to keep the peace, but to prevent and help to suppress disorder and law-breaking, and examples can be found in the documents describing the "hue and cry." The state of the roads and the amount of unpunished crime (particularly robbery) in the early part of the nineteenth century have been described in many novels, and some useful statistics are given in the *Encyclopaedia Britannica* under "Police." The introduction of a regular police force in London by Sir Robert Peel made a start towards better things. The Municipal Reform Act of 1835 saw the formation of municipal police; but, as it was permissive, many districts were still left unpoliced and worse off than before, because the felons whom the police discomfited in the towns swooped on the unpoliced districts. The year 1856 saw the formation of the County Police, and since then crime has decreased very greatly, and undetected crime has practically ceased to exist. The Bow Street Runners and the hateful system of Tyburn tickets have given way to the detective force with its headquarters at Scotland Yard. Our police system and our policemen gain the admiration of all the world.

The collection of material illustrative of this development is more difficult and much of the work must fall on the teacher, unless the school is fortunate enough to possess a good encyclopaedia.

(iii) *The Administration of Justice.*

This subject can be treated similarly, but any attempt to trace the chaos existing in our judicial system before the Judicature Act of 1873 would be too laborious and unin-

9—2

teresting for school purposes. It is not worth while as
knowledge, and would serve no useful function as training.
The chronic state of English justice, almost mocking Magna
Carta—"To none will we sell, deny, or delay justice"—can
be seen from the novels of Dickens. The Act of 1873 swept
away the anomalies and set up the present system, which is
the best and purest in the world.

From our point of view it is desirable that pupils should
gain some insight into the judicial system, and therefore
the pair working on this topic can be set to work, *A* reading
the chapter in *The Rights and Duties of the English Citizen*
whilst *B* reads Green's *Elementary Citizenship* (Longmans).
Then they can compare their notes and question each other.
For example, *A* asks *B*, "Suppose a man has been murdered,
what happens when the police hear?" *B* then gives the
answer, "Coroner's inquest, and arrest, if the person is
known; if unknown, the Coroner's jury bring in the verdict
'Wilful murder against some person unknown'." *B* asks *A*,
"When was the Coroner's office instituted?" If *A* does not
know, *B* gives the answer and gains a mark. He can also
ask a further question, such as: "Suppose a man is arrested
and charged with a serious offence, what checks are designed
to prevent his liberty being taken away?" The answer is as
follows:

1. Twelve men (*Coroner's Jury* for murders).
2. *Magistrate's Court,* where a preliminary enquiry is held, resulting
   in acquittal or in the accused being sent to a higher court.
3. *Quarter Sessions* (*jury*)—or, if too serious for sessions, as in the
   case of murder, arson, forgery, etc., prisoner sent to:
4. *Assizes,* where, if the Grand Jury return a true bill, he is tried
   by jury and, if sentenced, still has the right to appeal to:
5. *Court of Criminal Appeal*—appeal upheld, or appeal refused and
   the sentence confirmed, reduced, increased, or quashed. Even
   then the Crown has the prerogative of mercy (if Home Secretary
   recommends a reprieve).

In this way the pupils test one another and incidentally learn their topic. The pupils, on reporting to the master, can be further questioned. As a rule, if they have cross-questioned one another, they are well primed, but of course there are questions which would not occur to boys but which the master knows are too pertinent to be overlooked and which he would ask the pair, such as the following:

Why are Judges well paid?
Who appoints the Judges of the High Court? Who "recommends"?
Who appoints the Lord Chief Justice?
How can Judges be dismissed?
What departments of the High Court of Justice were set up by the Judicature Act?
Who *really* tries a man indicted of a serious criminal offence, Mr Justice So-and-So or the jury?
What happens if a man refuses to serve on a jury?
What cases are tried in the County Courts to-day?

This topic ought to show the improvement in the administration of justice. An account of a trial to-day compared with a trial a hundred years ago will do much to explode the "good old days" fallacy. Records may be found which will enable the pupils to compare a trial at the Old Bailey in 1820 with the trial and sentence of a man for a similar offence before the learned Recorder to-day at the Central Criminal Court. This shows a pupil better than anything else how the brutality of our criminal law has been mitigated and why English justice is the envy and admiration of the world.

(iv) *The Making of Laws.*

The Most High Court of Parliament is an august institution, full of interest; but, until a little while ago, the attention given to it at school was largely confined to a consideration of the extension of the franchise. The actual procedure in Parliament has changed very little, and the main outlines can be learned quickly, although the intricacies of party procedure may take years to learn.

The distinction between Bye (Byre) Laws, or *Town Laws*, and the Law of England (Statutes of the Realm) is best grasped by actual striking examples. The Common Law can also be illustrated by similar extracts (see C. R. L. Fletcher, *An Introductory History of England*, Chapter xiv). Pupils can be set to read *A Primer of English Citizenship*, Chapter iv, and *Parliament*, Chapter iii, by Sir C. P. Ilbert (Home University Library); also *The Rights and Duties of the English Citizen*, pp. 40 *et seq.* Having read these, the pair can question one another as before.

The record-book might well contain accounts of famous scenes and debates in Parliament, such as : Pitt's speeches against Walpole—the dagger scene (Fox and Burke)— Gladstone and Disraeli—the Irish turbulence—the Asquith speech on Declaration of War—the retirement of Mr Speaker Lowther—the election of the present Speaker (see *Times* Parliamentary Report)—etc.

Conclusion.

The other special topics can be treated in a similar way, so that the work of the term really prepares pupils for an intelligent grasp of the principles of citizenship and the structure of government through an understanding of the more recent developments in history.

PART III

SOME ECONOMIC ASPECTS OF SCHOOL GEOGRAPHY

"No one dreamed of the enormous potential productivity of material and moral energy alike, which proves to have been latent in the national being; it is for the national consciousness as a whole to direct that tide of energy into constructive work, and the near future of this national consciousness depends in great measure upon the efforts of teachers to apply, by continual reference and illustration, the lessons of the war to the wider lesson of social obligations as a whole. Opportunities for doing so in school work, not merely without irrelevance, but in integral connection with a number of school subjects, can be found in unexpected plenty by those who will take the trouble to seek them out."

KENNETH RICHMOND, *Education for Liberty.*

SOME ECONOMIC ASPECTS OF
SCHOOL GEOGRAPHY

IN a recent and comprehensive book on the teaching of geography, the science is defined as that which "deals with the sum total of human effort in relation to the environment in which human life is passed; school geography includes as complete a treatment of the science as opportunity and the limits of time permit[1]." Naturally, a subject so wide in its outlook and so comprehensive in its grasp must be greatly restricted before its content can be suitable for school purposes; and in the present chapter we intend to give special attention to those aspects of geographical study and training which are almost directly useful to pupils as citizens to be.

As in the teaching of history one saw that the greatest care and circumspection was necessary in selecting the most suitable and useful phases for study in school, so in the teaching of geography a similar quest is requisite. The teacher of geography, however, has this advantage over his colleague, that he feels it is possible to give a survey of the world as a whole, whereas the teacher of history knows he can never hope to give any adequate description of the story of man and of all the nations in the short span of school life. But granting this difference, and allowing for the differences which arise through the different perspective, teachers of both subjects experience similar difficulties. Each has to ask himself which aspects of the vast panorama that the subject enfolds are to be painted in detail, and

[1] B. C. Wallis, *The Teaching of Geography* (Cambridge University Press).

which ought to be lightly sketched in. Certainly an evenness of treatment would leave a vague and unconvincing impression of the subject.

Where can the teacher find a guide?

In dealing with questions of method, it is unfortunate that we rarely look back and survey the work in the past which is often so helpful in solving questions of to-day. Let us therefore try to outline the chief stages through which the teaching of geography has passed in the last three decades. The first stage—when geography was but grudgingly recognized as a school subject—showed a slavish devotion to names which were learnt by rote. The subject-matter for a typical lesson was the capes and bays of Great Britain, and quite tediously one learnt them off, beginning with some known point on the coast and "working round." The geography text-books of the more advanced "academies for the sons of gentlefolk" were often learnt by heart. Maps, with wonderful herring-bone mountains drawn freehand, were highly prized—the best of them evoked murmurs of delight from approving parents when "hung" in the school exhibition. The unfortunate pupil who could not "do" freehand was quite lost, and in consequence could hardly hope to "do" geography. Gradually better methods prevailed. It was pointed out that one does not necessarily know more about a thing by giving it a name, and the phase of "names, idle names" passed away, only to be followed by a period when physical geography—physiography with a dash of commercial geography—was most in favour. Drawings of volcanoes in action, clouds, and other natural phenomena held sway as outward signs of inward erudition. But physical, commercial, and political geography were regarded as separate subjects or often learnt from separate text-books. Gradually, however, the modern conception and practice of the subject swept away the previous ideas. Led by Sir Halford Mackinder, Dr Herbertson, and others, teachers have so improved the conception and practice of the subject that in the best schools to-day it really fulfils the claim to be "an essential element in the training of the numerically most important part of the future citizens and voters."

But apart from general improvement of practical teaching, what is the factor which has been most largely responsible for this change? Without doubt one can say "because to-day the world is regarded as *the home of man*." It is the human element which, present now, was lacking before. Scientific treatment and a recognition of the essential unity of the subject have played no mean part in the improvement. But the changed conception emphasizing the human element throughout every stage of the teaching (descriptive, transitional, and argumentative), is the vital factor. This gives the teacher of geography the right to claim that "for breadth of outlook, for intimate relation with the palpitating human life which surrounds the pupil, for an insight into the wonder-world of inanimate and animate objects, no school subject can compete with geography[1]."

Now for present purposes, if the subject is to justify the high claims of the best teachers, it must lead out into the world of to-day, giving pupils sound training and also a body of knowledge useful to them as citizens. The world must no longer be regarded as an object of curiosity, like some exhibit in the vast museum of the universe, but as the workshop, the playground, and the home of man—the conqueror, overcoming his geographic limitations, making the most of the advantages offered by his environment, and ceaselessly striving to lighten the burdens of his existence. Imagine the difference between two pupils, one who only

[1] B. C. Wallis, *op. cit.*, p. 13.

knew the position, size, configuration, climate, exports, etc. of New Guinea, and one who backed this by such reading as C. A. W. Monkton's *Some Experiences of a New Guinea Magistrate* and *Last Days in New Guinea.* One pupil has a body of knowledge which may be useful but which will soon be forgotten; the other has a mental picture of a virile race of savages emerging from cannibalism under English rule. He also gets some insight into the character of the type of men who uphold the honour of the flag and the English name, and, incidentally, of the type who would ruin the Empire if given a free hand.

Let us assume that the teacher has questioned himself and feels satisfied that in teaching he has:

1. Kept the human element always to the forefront;

2. Always recognized the essential unity of the subject;

3. Maintained a judicious balance between the various aspects of the subject—regional, physical, economic, and political; and that he has not unduly emphasized any aspect to the neglect of the human element;

4. Gathered as much suitable material as possible in order that the facts he requires his senior pupils to study and the theories he wishes to exemplify may be available for them, so that under his guidance they can pursue their enquiries to the end fully and thoroughly and gain real practice in the methods of geographical enquiry. These questions of "thoroughness" and "balance" are very important. Many schemes show a lack of balance and much geographical teaching a lack of thoroughness. The value of such thoroughness of geographical explanation can be seen from a perusal of Chapter VIII of *The Teaching of Geography* by B. C. Wallis, dealing with this question. It will be noticed that unless the instance given is dealt with thoroughly, the economic aspect of the teaching is neglected.

In this case, there would be little need for any teaching specially directed to ensure that pupils grasped the elementary laws of economics and the way in which they work. But even then, unless from the inception of the course the teacher takes care to keep in mind the economic lessons and truths he wishes to teach, there is a great danger that they will be overlooked or, what is perhaps more harmful, misunderstood through faulty presentation.

It is therefore necessary to outline the conception of Economic Geography, and to define the economic laws which can be taught through the medium of school geography.

1. In the earlier descriptive and transitional stages of teaching, the gradual victory of man over his environment should be brought out by examples, showing how man has advanced towards civilization and the steps he has taken, in the various stages of this advance, to supply and to satisfy his felt human wants—the elementary needs of human life (food and drink, raiment, housing, etc.). A study of the various types of life, aboriginal, hunting, pastoral, agricultural, and industrial, will show this[1].

2. Throughout the whole course, attention should be drawn to the origin and working of our present economic system, showing the importance, the true significance, and essential interdependence of:

A. **Natural resources** and facilities, such as fertility of soil, possession of useful minerals, accessibility to markets,

[1] The pastoral life with its wealth in flocks, the agricultural life with wealth in land, though studied as "types" in geography, ought to recall the similar lessons in history. The classification of landowners for military service in ancient Greece, the five hidemen, the knight's fee in England, the forty-shilling freeholder, and lastly the householder, all show man at various stages in their development towards modern industrial life, adapting his organizations and groupings in accordance with new conditions.

facility for inland transport, position relative to the world's highways, suitability of climate—in short, the importance and value of natural endowment and riches.

B. **Capital**, which must be shown as the re-invested savings of the thrifty people, with which labourers are maintained, land bought, and plant erected, etc., until the industry becomes productive of wealth, which, in its turn, is distributed. Capital is wealth which is helping to produce wealth, and its function in opening up and developing a " new " country must be brought out—*e.g.* the railways in South America, and the Assuan Dam, which might be compared with the Pyramids, giving an example of useful expenditure of modern capital as contrasted with non-productive expenditure of an earlier age. Teachers will find many other simple illustrations, which are especially useful if linked up with the pupil's knowledge of history or litera-ture ; such as :

(1) One of the earlier forms of capital is represented by the store of food on which villeins and small-holders subsisted until the harvest. This they must save (cf. the old English phrase of "putting by for a rainy day," which perhaps really meant a bad harvest; for the failure of the crop wiped out these little stores, a loss of capital which was sometimes complete). Then recourse was made to the store of the greater holder, the landlord, and thus the small-holders became dependent, because debtors of the richer folk. (Cf. history lessons : England before the Conquest—Commendation.)

(2) Robinson Crusoe, before he built a plough, had to hunt especi-ally hard and save up surplus food on which he could live whilst making his plough. Thus he used his less durable capital (food) to make his plough (more durable); and it can be seen that all capital is wealth used in the production of other wealth. Crusoe "invested" the food he had saved in his plough. Compare capital to build a railway or a mill to-day. Nearly all is spent in maintaining labourers whilst they are building the railway or the mill. It is *wealth*, and it is spent in wages and buying material (much of this goes ultimately in wages), and rent (the landowner's share), and interest (the thrifty people's share). It can then be seen that as long as people have stomachs and appetites capital must exist, and, whether it be given another name or not, it is an absolute essential to livelihood and progress.

C. **Labour.** The need for labour to support existence in all countries, but especially in the crowded temperate districts of the world, needs little emphasis; but the importance of labour and the need for skill, industry, and knowledge in the "working class" is exemplified in studying the geography of all modern industrial communities or regions. A comparison between the inhabitants of Spain and Lancashire brings out the importance of a skilled race of working people, and shows how environment has affected the work of the people, which, in its turn, has reflected and helped to stabilize the cotton industry in Lancashire, and has become an important factor in making it prosperous. Another point to which attention ought to be directed is that the brain of the inventor, the pen of the clerk, the industry and skill of the directors and managers, and the diligence of the overseers are just as much " labour "—just as essential to the prosperity of industry and commerce— as the muscle and sweat of the navvy and spade-man.

How are these ideas to be presented ? How can pupils be directed to see them without having recourse to the least convincing method of instruction, mere telling ? Two points are evident :

(*a*) That detailed enquiry such as this, which must be thorough and searching to be effective, is best deferred until the later stages of school life, when geographical explanation can be taken to its fullest extent.

(*b*) That, wherever possible, local examples should be used. For instance, children in a town where the copper-smelting industry is localized ought to know the geographical factors which determine and modify the industry. At present, most teachers of geography would content themselves with giving their pupils a geographical explanation in bare outline of the reasons for the localization of the industry. But even if the explanation is thorough, that does not go far enough. The lesson should not be considered complete without a visit to the works, if that is possible, or at any rate a lively description of the processes involved, and a consideration of factors like the following:

Where does the raw material come from? What sort of people mine it? Who export it—what ships carry it over the sea? Where is it unloaded and how forwarded to the works? How many sets of men handle the product? Where does the smelted copper go to after the "works" have finished with it? Who make it up into utensils and other articles of commerce, etc.? Supposing shipping costs are exorbitant, or one set of workmen can demand and get higher wages than the industry can bear, what effect does this have on:

    (i) the price of the finished articles;
   (ii) the cost of production;
  (iii) the sale of the goods;
  (iv) the general cost of living, etc.?

If copper was to be discovered nearer the works which could undersell the (let us say) Spanish ore, what would happen? Is it cheaper to send heavy raw material by sea or by land? Why is coal so essential and cheap coal so necessary to the prosperity of the industry?

If possible, a balance-sheet of the Company whose works were visited may be shown to the pupils. They will see that labour and management, coal and raw material are the chief items of expenditure; and it is evident that if the amount paid to labour is larger than the Company can afford, or if, for any reason, the industry ceases to become a paying concern, it must stop. Children of fourteen or fifteen years of age, having been directed to the number of men's hands through which the product has passed (and consequently kept them in employment), can easily see the distress and loss caused by the stoppage. They can also see for themselves that the greater the amount which the "works" produce or turn out, the more copper is mined, sold, handled, and transported. More employment thus means more prosperity and cheaper copper goods, which help along every other industry and even every man using copper—for instance, everybody who buys a copper kettle or puts an electric bell in his house, or goes on board a ship (for cheaper copper helps to make cheaper ships and cheaper freight and passenger rates)—and so on.

In this way, by thoroughness of enquiry and careful teaching, the laws of supply and demand, the importance of transport, the principles governing wages, etc., are outlined. The way is paved for a better understanding of the commercial and industrial nexus on which in overcrowded industrial communities we depend for our very existence, to say nothing of the comforts of civilized life. But it is only by careful preparation and well planned method that the fullest advantage can be gained from lessons like these. The enquiry must be thorough; it must be based on reality and on actual examples. There must be no straining, not even any re-orientation of the subject-matter, to demonstrate or exemplify an economic truth which does not arise from the material or the particular example being studied.

In lessons similar to the above, in which a particular industry is under study in order to bring out the practical effects of geographical conditions and the actual working of economic laws, the teachers of geography and history might collaborate, the latter giving an outline of the development of the industry, and the former dealing with the geographic reasons for its localization and also its state and working to-day. Pupils in Lancashire should realize the importance of the cotton industry not merely as a means of livelihood to Lancashire people, but as a prime factor in the wealth and prosperity of England. Similarly the children in the Sheffield district should be *au fait* with the steel and cutlery industry; in Widnes pupils should know about the chemical industry and, if possible, about the German competing industry—a most useful and instructive

s   10

comparison. It is not enough to know *why* an industry is localized; senior pupils must know how it works, where the chief competing foreign industries are situated, why they are able to compete so successfully against the home-town industry, and what circumstances or causes may ruin the local industry. It is the latter aspect which, if neglected, leads to the idea one hears expressed : " Well, whatever happens, we always have ' the works '." Therefore, in the senior forms, attention must be paid to those factors which can damage or wipe out industry, so nullifying geographic advantages and the value of natural resources : *e.g.* failure of the cotton crop.

3. Attention ought to be directed to the actual working of the simpler laws of economics through all stages of the teaching, and in the later years lessons should be chosen to demonstrate them more fully.

(i) *The Laws of Supply and Demand* and the principles which govern values and regulate prices[1] in the market. The expression that prices, wages, etc., are regulated by supply and demand is so common that it is often accepted as an explanation without being understood. The teacher must explain the laws governing supply and demand by examples, avoiding technical terms but at the same time making the matter quite clear to his pupils. As given by Jevons, the laws are : "A rise in price tends to produce a greater supply and a less demand; a fall of price tends to produce a less supply and a greater demand. Commercially an increase of supply or a decrease of demand tends to lower price, and a decrease of supply or an increase of demand to raise prices."

[1] Price means "the quantity of money one will give for a thing." Value means that so much of one thing is given for so much of another—it is a proportion; price is a measure—the money-measure of value.

Unless these laws are built up by pupils from examples, they are too difficult for non-adult minds to understand; but the youngest children can see from a single example, such as Brown exchanging some of his marbles with Jones for the latter's peg-top, that there must be a demand for Brown's marbles, and the number he will have to give (the barter) will vary according to the value in marbles which Jones puts on his top. If the supply of peg-tops was unlimited, the number of marbles Brown would have to give for the top would be less. If there were few peg-tops or Jones had the only one for sale, then Jones could ask and get the maximum number of marbles that Brown would give. In short, Jones could make a very good "swap." Again, if marbles were greatly in demand, Brown would be inclined to offer fewer for the top, and Jones to accept fewer, and less still if several other boys had tops which they were willing to part with or barter (a good supply in the market). When the news of Jones having made such a good "swap," or that he got such a high price for his top, gets round, other boys would be tempted to part with their tops; so the rise in price tends to bring about a greater supply and so on. Teachers will find that, as a rule, some bright boy raises the question of "fashion"—*i.e.* the fact that it was just because almost every other boy except Brown had a top which made him so keen to have one (to be "in the swim"). This puzzles the class, unless it is pointed out that this condition is not really a condition *of the market*, for, although boys are well supplied with tops, they are not willing to part with them because they are "all the go" at the time, and therefore supply in the market is very limited. It is only when tops go out of fashion, when demand decreases, that prices fall; and boys easily see this if one is careful to point out that a good supply

10—2

implies a good supply of tops *for sale* and not merely that there are "plenty about."

From a simple example like this one can easily pass to the laws fixing price and supply and demand in the market— say, a definite market where butter or any other commodity is sold. If the demand is keen and the supply is good, the price is such that the quantity demanded is equal to the quantity supplied. If the price is too high for people, they decide to wait and do not buy; then there is higgling or bargaining until agreement is reached, and if a price is not agreed on, no sale is effected. Demand may be there, in the sense that people will still want butter on their bread; but actually the market shows no demand and price comes down, or the farmers and sellers take their butter home. It often happens that, rather than take it back unsold, they sell at a reduced price. But, having found the demand "slack" one week, they bring less goods to market—having churned less butter—when they come again. Thus demand has reacted on supply. Consequently, this week, butter is "shorter" than usual and the purchasers get anxious, and so more can be asked and got by the sellers—so butter goes up in price. In this way, when a woman selling chickens or poultry asks her neighbour "how are your chickens going to-day?", meaning how are they selling and what price are they "fetching," she is really giving an example of the constant enquiry about the relative state of supply and demand which is typical of the whole commercial world.

As teachers, we have to do our best to ensure that elementary principles like these, which are understood quite easily when relative to simple deals or "swaps," are understood when they operate in the open market—not necessarily a place or market-ground, but wherever supply meets or equals demand—and between the great firms of different nations. Even between employers and employees the same laws hold good, but the operation of supply and demand in regulating wages is complex; the questions of a living wage, of the influence of State interference, and the regulation and restriction of Trades Unions, if touched on at all, can only be dealt with in the senior forms and then quite lightly. The conclusions must be the conclusions the pupils draw for themselves under direction, and ought to arise from the study of a particular example or the working of a particular industry.

(ii) *The Laws regulating International Trade* ought to be understood. When pupils realize that exchange consists in giving the comparatively superfluous for the comparatively necessary (the basis of all trade), and understand the meaning of "value" and "price," then they can see that, although trade, *i.e.* exchange, does not produce or create material wealth, it really *increases* wealth, because it transfers the material to places where it has greater usefulness (utility); where it satisfies a more keenly felt want, and where the demand for it is consequently greater than in the place from which it was transferred by commerce. Thus England has surplus coal, and this is exchanged with other countries which need coal for goods of which they have a surplus and of which we in turn feel the want. "Two nations cannot enter upon an enduring foreign trade with one another unless the comparative values of things in the one country differ from the comparative values of the same things in the other country."

Take the case of Russia, which gives the teacher ot geography an opportunity of explaining the theory of foreign trade perhaps more clearly than any other country, because, before the war, Russia and England were economically and commercially complementary to each other to a greater extent than any other two countries. Let us take the pre-war trade in wheat from Russia and in agricultural implements and machinery from England. The surplus wheat Russia produced had a greater actual value in England, where it was no longer surplus to the requirements of the population, than in Russia; the agricultural machinery which was made in England, surplus to English requirements, had a greater value in Russia than here; hence it was profitable to both countries to exchange wheat for machinery and trade flourished. If Germany or any other country—for other countries will enter the market set up by this trade—can deliver machinery as good as ours at a cheaper rate than ours, then the Germans must capture that market, and the English trade must reduce the cost of production (of the delivered goods) so as to beat the Germans, or English trade in those goods will cease. The margin between the "tenders" put in by the competing countries is naturally small if (as is usual) competition is keen, and it may be a very slight rise in wages, in the cost of insurance, or of transport (freights and porterage) which just makes the difference and causes the trade to be no longer worth while. The difference between the comparative values of the commodities in the two countries would be so slight that the trader could not make any profit; therefore trade stops, for to trade at a loss is against human nature and economic laws.

The state of Russian trade to-day might well be examined, because this is an outstanding example of natural wealth and resources being rendered almost valueless by the mistakes and folly of mankind in the War and after. It shows (i) the value of a stable government and national credit; (ii) the importance of transport, railways, rolling stock, engines, etc.; (iii) that an immense fall in production results in no surplus, no exchange value, no exports, and no imports, unless paid for in bullion, which is a ruinous form of international payment.

These are simple cases, but in school we must confine ourselves to simple cases. Of course, there is the question of tariffs and subsidies to "protect" or to help industries; which may be temporary expedients or part of a deliberate policy; and whether the subject can be treated in schools is a moot point. At any rate, in schools it is not desirable to go beyond a knowledge of what tariffs, protective duties, and subsidies are, and the reasons given for their imposition or grant. The effect of protective import duties and of subsidies on our industry and commerce is still a vexed political question, rather hypothetical and unsuited to the non-adult mentality. It is well left outside the content of economic geography in our schools.

(iii) *The Laws of Increasing and Diminishing Returns*, as principles, are too difficult to be understood by the average youth even in senior classes, but if practical examples are given, their general workings can be understood.

As stated by Professor Chapman, they are:

"The law of increasing returns affirms that an increase of the productive factors devoted to any manufacture is usually accompanied, in the long run, by a more than proportionate return, meaning a lower cost of production."

"The law of decreasing returns declares that, after a time, any attempt to add to the supplies of natural products will meet with less ample returns, in the absence of improvements in productive methods."

Let us take the farming industry in England during the war. England only grew enough food to supply herself for about one day a week. When the attempted blockade by submarines began, there was a great outcry for more land to be brought under cultivation. A farmer in peace time had naturally cultivated his best land—his most accessible land—first. During the war he was made to till even the outlying and less fertile fields, and naturally they brought him in less returns, causing his average return per acre to be lowered, raising his costs of production, etc. Naturally this would cause a rise in the price of food, in spite of all precautions governments and administrators might take. How can this tendency be restrained? Only by improved methods of farming and more intensive culture. Hence the importance of tractors and improved agricultural methods, and, incidentally, the dismay of the officials when the Germans sank ship after ship containing huge consignments of tractor-ploughs in 1917.

The reasons for the law of increasing returns are more simple. As a business grows and gets established, it can afford better machinery; it can pay better wages, thereby attracting better workmen; it can specialize and reap the benefit from its subsidiary industries, and so on. Therefore it will yield increasing returns—it *might* even lower the prices of the goods it makes and still show increasing returns.

Pupils can easily see that there is a point beyond which it is not possible to go. Children familiar with the woollen industry can see that more capital and energy put into a business will, as a rule, bring more trade and industry to that mill; but that a point is reached—and it varies with the particular state of the industry in general and that branch of it in particular—when the extra outlay will not bring in increasing returns, but rather the opposite.

In this way, by simple illustration pupils can see that developments in industry are not the outcome of caprice, but are governed by the interaction of economic laws.

(iv) *The Distinction between Money and Wealth* must be thoroughly understood.

Wealth has been variously defined—Jevons describes it as the term under which we comprehend "all those things …which are transferable, are limited in supply, and are directly or indirectly productive of pleasure or preventive of pain." Professor Chapman writes: "wealth is what people want to satisfy their needs, directly or indirectly, and have to spend time and effort in getting."

Money, on the other hand, must be shown as a recognized medium of exchange and as a measure of value, giving a common standard to the amount or proportions agreed on in "barter," and doing away with the difficulties which would hinder exchange without some recognized medium. The money value in exchange is called the price. Now as money is a measure, it is easy to see that the best measure —the best material for money—is some desirable commodity which itself does not easily fluctuate in price. Hence the adoption of gold and silver, which have the further advantage of being easily carried about, are not easily destroyed[1], and are more hygienic than most substances.

The difference between wealth and money can be exemplified by showing that the effect of increasing the money in a country really tends to make prices rise—that is, to make wealth (things desirable) more difficult to obtain because there are more bidders and more money is offered than before—and, in a way, to make people poorer. This has already been shown in the history course during the reign of Edward VI, when the vast influx of Spanish-American gold and silver lowered the value of gold and helped, among other things, to make prices higher and, in so far as

[1] Reference might be made to "chipping" and "debasing" in earlier ages.

the stabilizing powers of prices are considered, to keep them high. It is just as true to-day. Even if England printed enough paper money to allow everyone £1000 per week, wealth would not have increased, and therefore we should be no better off. In fact, all production is producing wealth—otherwise it dies out; and the chief factor in the increase of our wealth must necessarily be this production —the output of things which satisfy human wants, which are transferable (able to be exchanged), limited in supply, and useful.

In dealing with the natural resources—the country's natural endowment with those commodities which are most useful and which can be turned into wealth by human fore-sight and labour—the teacher gets many opportunities to drive home these distinctions and to emphasize the difference between money and wealth, and the importance of the industry of the people, which alone can turn natural riches into wealth. Air is not wealth, because it is unlimited in supply; but on the other hand the temperature or humidity of the air may be helping or hindering factors in the pro-duction of wealth. Health and happiness, laughter and the love of friends, the most desirable things, are not wealth, because they are not actually transferable; but on the other hand the services of a footman, cook, policeman, tinker, teacher, or doctor can all be regarded as wealth. They are transferable, limited in supply, and useful—in short, they can be bought.

Arising out of the study of the comparative value of various natural resources, the case of coal and iron mines as compared with gold and silver mines in determining the wealth of a country affords an opportunity of showing that gold mines and silver mines do not of themselves make a country wealthy. For instance, coal and iron will be used to make other wealth; industry and commerce will be attracted to the country with coal and iron. But the richest gold or silver mining areas in the world may still remain "up-country settlements[1]" (cf. Klondike, Baroda, and the State of Nevada to-day). Examples like these tend to drive home in the minds of pupils the true factors constituting the wealth of a country.

How far other economic ideas, such as the part played by labour in causing values, and the question of trade depressions and their recurrence, can be dealt with depends upon the particular teacher and the class. It would be very unwise to give a "set" lesson on these questions, but from time to time opportunities occur—such as, for example, the effect of the failure of the American cotton crop or a bad harvest—which enable a teacher to discuss these things informally with the greatest advantage.

Unfortunately it is true that many teachers to-day regard instruction in the simple truths and ideas of economics, or an enquiry into the workings of an industry such as are outlined above, as quite beyond the scope of school geography or school study at all. But surely it is to our interests as citizens, and our duty as teachers, to realize that we must act as liaison officers between pupils in school and the outside world. It is in the interests of our pupils that they should understand the part they will have to play in the world of industry and commerce; and it is to the employer's interest and to that of every citizen in the community to have youths "start work" knowing something of the industry, and, if possible, of the firm, in which they begin their careers. The school is the place for this kind

---

[1] *E.g.* All boys who have read *Montezuma's Daughter* will realize that gold was perhaps more plentiful then in Mexico than in any other country before or since. Were the Aztecs rich *because* of this?

of teaching. Economic laws are inviolable and ignorance of them becomes more dangerous each year, because each year the world of commerce and industry becomes more technical and more delicately balanced, and a small body of men—even one or two—can upset that balance, causing industrial disputes of far-reaching consequences. These disputes would often be avoided if the disputing parties could foresee the economic consequences of such action. As we stated in the introduction, the teacher's share in the general improvement which must take place may easily be over-estimated; but, for all that, truth is truth, and honest instruction which will be accepted and learnt from a fair-minded and respected teacher, will be rejected and ignored as self-interested and fallacious from the mouth of an equally fair-minded employer. It is clear that the school which fails to give this instruction neglects its duty to the community in the training of citizens.

PART IV

TRAINING IN SELF-GOVERNMENT

"Instruction in matters of moral import is ineffective everywhere when it is not combined with practical exercise or custom. In this point of exercise and custom the public schools of England and the colleges of Oxford and Cambridge are far in advance of us. We Germans always believe that we can effect all school education by means of explanations by words or book, through mere lectures and addresses of all kinds. That is certainly the most convenient and the cheapest method of public education.... The training of a people demands more."

GEORG KERSCHENSTEINER, *The Schools and the Nation.*

TRAINING IN SELF-GOVERNMENT

THE creation of a sound public sentiment, even in the later years of school life, is a difficult task. The training, discipline, and tone of the school all tend to induce habits of loyalty, co-operation, and public spirit. This is especially the case if some form of self-government is operative in the school; for unless the pupils have some outlet for the inborn gift of self-government so marked in British school-boys, the seeds of the right spirit, though they may be sown, are merely sown by the wayside. Any scheme of civic instruction which does not make provision for self-government loses much of its value, and schools must make some attempt to grapple with this problem. Certain it is to-day that many boys who were full of the right spirit at school, and for whom the good of the school was the supreme law, fail to apply this community-spirit to the community at large when they become citizens. This is unfortunate, and probably due to the fact that much of modern education is out of touch with life; but, in a measure, it is due to the absence of opportunity for self-government in the schools themselves. In some schools everything is done *for* the pupils; they have little or no chance to do anything for themselves. While this state of things may be necessary in the few schools where control is conscious of its weakness, it is always unfortunate. Even in schools which are well staffed and where the tone is good, many little duties and much supervision are done by the teaching staff which could with advantage be done by the pupils themselves[1].

---

[1] *E.g.* Supervision in playground and in ablution rooms and corridors, etc.

Some little organization is necessary to initiate schemes; but it is well worth while, for it helps to make pupils realize that the school is "their show," and this is the spirit which must be engendered and encouraged before any movement towards freer discipline or self-government can be completely successful. Every opportunity to encourage the community-sense must be taken in Hall and in class-room, for the growth of specialization and of specialists tends to break down the feeling of "oneness" in school, and this tendency must be countered in every possible way. In this respect it is much to be regretted that gatherings of the whole school are becoming less frequent. In many schools these gatherings in Hall are being curtailed and squeezed out of the time-table. The pressure of examinations, the general acceleration of the pace of school life, and the multiplication of school activities all need careful watching, lest there should be any tendency to crowd out, say, the school ceremony which opens or closes the week. The importance of these ceremonies, when they are well conducted[1], can hardly be over-estimated.

Schools, on the whole, are very conservative communities. They move slowly and suspect change. This is wise; it makes for stability and sound progress; but many headmasters who know that the tone and discipline in their schools are good, instead of feeling that the school is ready for some allocation of self-government, are rather inclined to leave well alone. So it is only to be expected that the change in schools, which the change to complete democracy in the nation seems to make necessary, will be slow and tentative.

[1] Such a small matter as encouraging the best readers (not only among the seniors) to read the Bible in Hall to the whole school at prayers reacts on the tone of the school (and the spoken English!) more than seems possible at first glance.

The amount of self-government that can with safety be allowed to pupils depends on so many factors that no rule can be formulated or laid down, for when all the schemes which have been tried are analyzed it is found that they owe their success in a large measure to the master in charge. However much he may withdraw himself, his personality and the strength of his good-will and direction are the guiding, if not the vital, factors. Further, he alone knows his boys and the inside working of his scheme, and therefore self-government in the school or class-room is a matter for research and cautious experiment at present. It is doubtful if it can ever be standardized in any way, and certainly the absence of any outside restrictions or regulations will be helpful rather than the reverse, because so much depends on the master that he must be given a free hand so that he in turn can give his scheme and the boys a fair trial. Therefore it is not proposed to enlarge on these topics, because direction and help are best given by the courageous few who have initiated schemes of self-government in their schools and class-rooms. But, apart from the possibilities of such schemes as elected prefects, prefects' courts, form-moots, class committees, competitive or "side" systems in school work, there are some points which are easily overlooked and which must be kept in mind, as they are essential in that all schemes of self-government must be based on them.

Firstly, in all school-work care must be taken to ensure that there is constant scope for individual effort on the part of the pupil, and that such effort is actually put forth. Facility for learning is easily confused with intelligence and sometimes with education itself, but it must be remembered that nimbleness of brain and retentiveness of memory sometimes go with suppleness and even weakness of character. Teachers will soon have to ask themselves if, in their desire to "get pupils on," to use the best and so-called "new" methods, they are not taking the heart out of education and in danger of making everything too easy for the pupil. The trend of methodology, the growth of specialisation, the advertisement of examination successes and the undue weight attached to them in the public mind, all tend in this direction. The danger of talking down to pupils, of over-explanation and over-direction, and of hyper-puerile methods generally, which cram the memory and atrophy the intelligence, is that they neglect the chief opportunity which schooling affords for the training of character. Unless boys are taught to try for themselves, to be self-reliant, and to form the habit of tackling work which seems difficult throughout their school life, it will not be possible to entrust them with any measure of self-government, because their schooling has vitiated rather than developed the very traits in their characters upon which self-government relies for success.

The gift of a bat does not make a boy a cricketer any more than the gift of the vote makes a man a citizen. It is the effective use of the bat or vote which decides the issue, and it is out of individual effort that true education emerges. Therefore care must be taken that at every stage the children have work to do, something to bite at that is difficult but just not too difficult for them[1]. The boy who rises from a low place in his form to a high place is "getting" education, and is more worthy of reward than the boy who is naturally gifted and usually at the top of the form. It is to be regretted that the trier is not more frequently rewarded, for his is the true distinction[2]. The inequality of

[1] See J. Fairgrieve, *The New Teaching,* p. 262.
[2] Does this account for the numbers of men now famous who were quite undistinguished at school?

natural endowment, so obvious in life, is often neglected in schools, not because teachers do not realize it, but because the present system does not make allowance for its gradation. The success of the Dalton Plan is a most welcome sign that this fact is recognized, and though casual and thoughtless observers may dub it a "go-as-you-please system," it is really a "go-as-hard-as-you-can" method, and highly valuable from the point of balancing the training of character and the grading of intelligence or natural endowment. To go further into these questions would lead too far into the making of character and would be outside the scope of this book; but in every phase of school life the sense of personal responsibility for a task or theme must be brought home to the pupil. He must be made to feel that it is "up to him," and although it may be helpful to sublimate the natural *ego* in a boy by making him work for his "side" in class, yet in the world at large, as a man, he will not get many opportunities to work for a side, but will work for himself and must take a pride in his work and stand or fall by it. Happily, as a result of a deeper study of industrial psychology, enlightened employers are giving men more opportunities to work for a side—a shed or a department; but at present a man works largely for himself, and if education is to be brought more closely into touch with life, educators cannot afford to forget it.

Secondly, the influence on citizenship of improved oral expression in the mother tongue will be great. If the school is to be brought into touch with life and to be a real training-ground for citizenship, this is perhaps the foremost need. Once we can turn out from our schools youths who are not tongue-tied but can express themselves clearly (even if not fluently) in simple English, the effect on civic life will be most marked. That much can be confidently asserted, because many who would gladly serve the locality or the county to-day hold back, not so much from ignorance of the working of the administration, lack of inclination, or lack of business capacity, but from the disability of oral expression and that dumbness which, until recently, the schools did little or nothing to overcome[1].

Thirdly, all pupils should know the rules of procedure which regulate a public meeting or discussion. Many a sound observation or helpful suggestion remains unsaid because of the average citizen's fear of being "out of order," or, as he would say, of making a fool of himself. These rules of procedure are a valuable part of a citizen's equipment, and all youths (and teachers) ought to be made familiar with the duties of the chairman, proposer, and seconder, and with proposal, amendment, previous question, point of order, casting vote, etc. Opportunities can be found in plenty for teaching these things in the English lessons without irrelevance by means of debates, mock trials, etc., so improving the spoken English and at the same time forming a valuable training for public service.

Over-enthusiastic advocates of self-government in schools are sometimes inclined to forget that a school which is too much in advance of the world is just as much out of touch with life as one which is too far behind the times. The danger of making schools utopian is too remote to discuss, but it would be unfortunate if, in the perfection of school administration and method, teachers were ever likely to forget that pupils are being prepared not for Utopia, but for citizenship in England as it is to-day, and that in many

---

[1] See Tomkinson, *The Teaching of English* (Oxford University Press) and Sampson, *English for the English* (Cambridge University Press); also the stress laid on oral expression in the *Report on the Teaching of English in England*.

respects life for pupils will be no primrose path to freedom.

In weighing up the possibilities of any device or scheme for the allocation of self-government to pupils, the average school-boy and the average citizen must be the standard, and for this reason an excellent rule is to ask, "has this scheme any counterpart in our national life?" If so, it has been tested by average citizens and is entitled to respect and a fair trial in school.

Let us take four examples from the methods recommended to promote self-government in schools and apply this test.

1. The prefects' court.
2. The election of prefects by the scholars.
3. The election of a form committee and speaker in the form-moot.
4. The control and setting of home-work by the pupils through their form committees.

Prefects' courts have been working quite successfully in some schools for many years. In one school, with which the writer is familiar, the court sits every Friday after school, the bench usually consisting of three prefects, who try offenders. The duty-master for the week may or may not be present; he is always within call, but usually keeps out of the way as much as possible. The offenders are all those who have lost conduct marks (of which the pupils have a fixed number to their credit each week) and also those who have repeatedly lost routine marks, and who are sent up to the court by the form committees (cf. sent to assizes). As a rule all minor offences—slackness, forgetfulness, occasional unpunctuality, and such-like breaches of order—are punished by the loss of routine marks, whereas cribbing, constant disorder, inattention, or discourtesy result in loss of conduct marks. The ratio might well be three

11—3

routine marks equal one conduct mark, though the marks are not interchangeable.   At the court, the speakers of the forms appear in order to present the offenders, who, if they have any reasonable defence, may bring witnesses or ask for a "prisoner's friend" (cf. court martial).   However, as a rule, they submit to the verdict and sentence of the court, because they know it to be a fair and just tribunal.   After a fair hearing the court passes sentence—either caution, admonition, or punishment (impositions or strokes), and the duty-master of the week then carries out the sentence. Boys, for whom the ordinary "licking" has no terrors and is no deterrent from misconduct, hate this court, for the prefects and all concerned take themselves most seriously, and the punishment awarded by the court is invariably more severe than that which a master would give under ordinary conditions.   The system can be recommended because it has a wholesome effect on the tone of the school, and further it has its counterpart in the outside world. The prefects are like the justices of the peace, and the whole court resembles the petty sessions; but its power and authority come from the fact that it is really a court of public opinion as interpreted by the best minds in the school.   It awakens the community-spirit and tends to show that misconduct and disorder are not merely offensive to the masters, but a nuisance to all the members of the school community.   In one school, where the tone is excellent and the standard of discipline high, these courts have been held for nearly ten years and there has scarcely been a single appeal from the judgement of the court to the headmaster, who, of course, is the ultimate court of appeal.

The second question—the election of prefects—presents more difficulty.   If all members of the school had a vote, and even if candidature for election was restricted to the senior forms, would the boys themselves know who was best fitted for the post? The school captain may be most popular and yet not the most suitable. Again, if the heads (or the elected speakers) of the forms were given prefect's rank, this would lead to trouble, for no junior should ever be invested with power to "tell off" a senior—it is bad for both and for the school; and no boy ought to be expected to command until he has learned to obey. The danger of making prigs is too obvious to be serious, but the system of elective prefects seems to run the risk of investing the wrong fellows and also of making prigs. Further, there is no parallel in outside life, for happily we do not elect our policemen, magistrates, or judges. It may be argued that boys who have elected a fool or knave at school to a position of authority are much less likely to make the same mistake in after life. There is perhaps some truth in this; but the school has too much to lose from bad prefects to leave anything to chance, and on the whole the experiment can hardly be recommended with confidence.

The third point to be tested is the election of a form committee and a chairman or speaker, who will act for the form. This has much to commend it, for the opportunities and scope for helpful co-operation between the master and the boys increase each year. It makes communal praise— and punishment—possible, and gives to the form an appearance of unity, out of which unity itself often springs. The spokesman is usually appointed for a term; he reports any difficulty to the master, and is generally responsible for his form mates. In this capacity he attends the prefects' court and meetings of the school council[1] to decide and

---

[1] Usually the head, house-masters, prefects, games captains, and the speakers.

make arrangements for school activities—sports, swimming galas, concerts, speech days, "tea-fights," parents' days, etc. All this is most helpful, and has its counterpart in English local government, for the representative is the Mayor, or Chairman, of his class, who feel that they are represented and see to it that the speaker really does them credit.

But when it is advocated that the form committee be given power to set and control home-work, doubts arise as to the advisability of such a scheme. Although it must be admitted that, given the right spirit and the right boys, they could be trusted to set and control their home-work, or even their school-work, yet is it wise to allow them to do this in view of the fact that in after life they will not be able to choose their jobs? Tasks are set by masters, the day's work varies with business which must be attended to, whether one "feels like it" or not; and therefore it seems a sounder plan to set the tasks for boys and to encourage them to do them cheerfully and thoroughly, because this is a sounder preparation for happy and contented citizenship.

There is little doubt that the reluctance shown by headmasters to initiate and experiment with schemes of self-government is largely due to the fear that the tone or discipline of the school will suffer in consequence. Most schoolmasters are almost abnormally conservative and have a wholesome dread of anything that savours of the crank or faddist. But what is the tone of a school? It is hard to define, but, however it may be defined, the communal effect of the self-control and self-respect of the members of the community is the ultimate factor. This self-control, which shows itself in thought for others and in thought for the school, is the only sound basis of good and decent discipline. Self-control implies repression, and in normal boys this is especially true because the *ego* is stronger in them than in adults. It is foolish to say that repression is non-educational, as some self-styled psychological experts have done, for at some stage or other there must be conscious and deliberate repression of feelings, emotions, and desires. Naturally this repression or inhibition is less noticed as one becomes older and more disciplined, because it is more habitual; but it is not less strong than in the early stage because its operation does not call for volitional activity. Good discipline, as we understand it in schools, is not repression from without but the play of self-control which comes from within. Years ago a master who could repress his class, or, as he would say, control it, was considered a good disciplinarian. Doubtless there are times when resort must be made to this active repression on the master's part; but the test of a teacher's disciplinary powers to-day is that he has rarely to resort to this extreme, because his discipline leads his pupils to control themselves by giving them scope and opportunity for self-control, so that they behave from habit, and become an ordered community rather than a community which is ordered about. It is not so much "I can control my class" as "Can your class control themselves?" A generous allocation of self-government enlarges the pupils' scope and opportunity for self-control and therefore it is most valuable, not only in raising the tone and developing a community-spirit, but as a preparation for citizenship. It is the finest discipline for peace, just as military training and drill as laid down in *Infantry Training* and worked out by English officers are the finest discipline in the world for war. Military discipline is a method of inducing self-control—a quick and thorough method, but it can easily result in a uniformity of action or a uniform repression of action[1] which, though it induces self-control,

[1] Thus, although the ultimate test of the discipline of a battalion

does so at the expense of initiative and, in a measure, of intelligence. The basic qualities to which it appeals and on which it relies are, however, the same as in school discipline —self-control, loyalty, and persistence of effort. School discipline as a preparation for peace must be a compromise; but if it reduces the outside repression and gives training and practice in self-control through the medium of self-government, it is the highest form of discipline; and the tone of the school must be improved rather than weakened by a judicious allocation of the means of self-government to pupils, because it helps to create a sound public sentiment and to promote the feeling that the good of the school is the supreme law.

It is not proposed to enlarge on the various means by which self-government may be granted in schools, for the danger of half stating a case, of minimizing difficulties or exaggerating success, is great. But the number of successful schemes in operation shows that the matter is worthy of the serious attention of responsible teachers, however cautious, however conservative. Naturally the amount of self-government varies greatly with the school and the pupils themselves, but one fact is certain—that if pupils are given powers in the right spirit they rarely abuse them. On the whole, boys are more strict in quelling disorder and in detecting and correcting slackness than the masters themselves, and after the preliminary trouble in launching a scheme of self-government, and the anxious time which comes when the novelty has worn off and the unruly spirits have failed in their attempts to wreck the scheme, it will be found that better order and a better tone prevail than

is its conduct in the face of the enemy, such outward signs as smartness, cheerfulness, absolute stillness on parade (repression of action) are not only part of the discipline, but also most reliable criteria of the standard of discipline attained.

under the *régime* of benevolent repression. But, above all these advantages, this early training in self-government at school forms a most valuable apprenticeship for civic duties in the larger community, the State. It stimulates leadership and initiative, often giving those who are dull at lessons a chance to show their worth and to reveal qualities which otherwise would have remained not only latent but dormant, and which in time will fit them to become worthy citizens of the British Commonwealth of Nations.

NOTES ON THE REPORTS OF THE BRITISH ASSOCIATION'S COMMITTEE ON "TRAINING IN CITIZENSHIP"

(Presented at Cardiff, 1920, and Edinburgh, 1921.)

The British Association Committee on Training in Citizenship has issued a Report containing a comprehensive syllabus of civics. The earlier Report groups the many topics of citizenship under twenty-one headings, namely : (1) The Origin of the State, (2) The History of Civilization, (3) Citizenship, (4) Monarchy and Democracy, (5) Central Government, (6) Local Government, (7) The Administration of Justice, (8) The Police and Public Safety, (9) Public Health, (10) Life Assurance and Pensions, (11) Education, (12) National Defence, (13) The British Empire, (14) National Unity, (15) Patriotism, (16) Industry and Commerce, (17) International Relations, (18) The Press, (19) Housing, (20) Temperance, (21) Leisure and Recreation. A closer reading of the syllabus issued by the Committee will show how much of the matter there outlined and suggested can be taught through the medium of existing school subjects. Parts II and III of this work, if analyzed, point out how this can be done without irrelevance, special pleading, or undue re-orientation of the existing syllabus. Some matters, such as those included under Temperance (20)—Prohibition in U.S.A., Local Option, etc.—have been deliberately left alone by the writer, firstly because in his opinion they are outside the scope of school-work, and secondly because no sound educational method can be suggested for teaching such topics. In these and similar matters a school is well advised either to leave their discussion to voluntary societies, if such happily exist, or to rely on the excellence of the Boy Scout scheme (see p. 18 of the Report of the Committee... British Association, Cardiff, 1920), which inculcates "Health and strength '*Through Practice of...*' and responsibility for personal hygiene, continence, temperance, physical development, games, etc." That is sound and practical—in short, true education ; whereas pious exhortation fails with the average boy, as with the average citizen ; and although it is not in the least suggested that so learned and eminent a body as the Committee of the British Association for the Advancement of Science recommend pious exhortation, yet from the nature of these subjects, the state of English public opinion at the present time, and the absence of trustworthy evidence, it is certain that most teachers would have to resort to special pleading, which is most undesirable and an abuse of the teacher's privileged position.

A SHORT LIST OF USEFUL BOOKS

1. CITIZENSHIP.

Sir Henry Jones, *Principles of Citizenship* (Macmillan).

Professor John MacCunn, *The Ethics of Citizenship* (Macmillan).

Maxwell Garnett, *Education and World Citizenship* (Cambridge Univ. Press).

Georg Kerschensteiner, *Education for Citizenship* (Harrap), *The Schools and the Nation* (Macmillan).

John D. Hunt, *The Dawn of a New Patriotism* (Macmillan).

British Association—Report of the Committee on "Training in Citizenship" presented at Cardiff, 1920 ; also Report presented at Edinburgh, 1921.

2. HISTORICAL.

F. S. Marvin, *The Living Past,* a sketch of Western Progress (Oxford Univ. Press).
>The most helpful book of recent times to teachers of history. Gives balance and breadth of outlook, emphasizing the growth of a common humanity and organized knowledge applied to social ends.

F. S. Marvin, *The Century of Hope* (Oxford Univ. Press).
>A general survey of the progress of the nineteenth century.

Gilbert Slater, *The Making of Modern England* (Constable).
>An attempt to trace the main features of the life of the nation during the last century.

H. J. Trail, *Social England* (Cassell).

Lowes Dickinson, *The Greek View of Life* (Methuen).

W. Warde Fowler, *The City States of Greece and Rome* (Macmillan).

A. E. Zimmern, *The Greek Commonwealth* (Oxford Univ. Press).

Woodrow Wilson, *The State* (Heath).

Sir Frederick Pollock, *Introduction to the History of the Science of Politics* (Macmillan).

J. B. Bury, *History of the Freedom of Thought* (Home Univ. Library).

Sir Courtenay P. Ilbert, *Parliament* (Home Univ. Library).

P. Meadows, *English Constitutional History* (Bell).

E. Jenks, *Parliamentary England* (Story of the Nations).

Keatinge and Frazer, *An Introduction to World History* (A. & C. Black).

A. J. Grant, *Greece in the Age of Pericles* (Methuen).

Edward A. Hughes, *Britain and Greater Britain in the Nineteenth Century* (Cambridge Univ. Press).

Marjorie and C. H. B. Quennell, *A History of Everyday Things in England* (Batsford).

3. SOCIOLOGICAL.

Benjamin Kidd, *The Science of Power*.

Maciver, *The Community*.

Graham Wallas, *The Great Society* (Macmillan).

J. J. Findlay, *An Introduction to Sociology* (Manchester Univ. Press).

4. USEFUL BOOKS FOR COMPARATIVE CIVICS.

Thomas Harrison Reed, *Form and Functions of American Government* (Harrap).

Edward M. Sait, *Government and Politics of France* (Harrap).

Woodrow Wilson, *Constitutional Government in the United States* (Oxford Univ. Press).

A. L. Lowell, *Greater European Governments* (Oxford Univ. Press).

5. ECONOMICS AND INDUSTRIAL HISTORY.

Marshall, *Economics of Industry*.

Charles Gide, *Principles of Political Economy* (Harrap).

S. J. Chapman, *Elementary Economics* (Longmans).
     A most useful introduction.

Sir W. Stanley Jevons, *Political Economy* (Macmillan's Science Primers).

Oxford Tracts on Economic Subjects, 1920 (Oxford Univ. Press).

H. O. Meredith, *Economic History of England* (Pitman).

Townsend Warner, *Tillage, Trade and Invention* (Blackie).

H. de B. Gibbins, *The Industrial History of England* (Methuen).

Sir Laurence Gomme, *The Village Community* (Scott), *The Making of London* (Oxford Univ. Press).

Sir T. H. Penson, *The Economics of Everyday Life* (Cambridge Univ. Press).

6. EDUCATION.

K. J. Freeman, *The Schools of Hellas* (Macmillan).

J. W. Adamson, *A Short History of Education* (Cambridge Univ. Press).

C. H. Birchenough, *A History of Elementary Education in England and Wales* (University Tutorial Press).

R. L. Archer, *Secondary and Higher Education in the Nineteenth Century* (Cambridge Univ. Press).

7. THE TEACHING OF HISTORY, GEOGRAPHY, AND CIVICS.

R. L. Archer, L. V. D. Owen, and A. E. Chapman, (1) *The Teaching of History in Elementary Schools*, (2) *The Teaching of Geography in Elementary Schools* (A. & C. Black).

Henry E. Bourne, *The Teaching of History and Civics in the Elementary and the Secondary School* (Longmans).

William Boyd, *The Teaching of Citizenship* in "The Modern Teacher" (Methuen).

H. B. Madeley, *History as a School of Citizenship* (Oxford Univ. Press).

Eugene L. Hasluck, *The Teaching of History* (Cambridge Univ. Press).

B. C. Wallis, *The Teaching of Geography* (Cambridge Univ. Press).

F. J. C. Hearnshaw, *The Teaching of History* in "The Modern Teacher" (Methuen).

M. W. Keatinge, (1) *Studies in the Teaching of History* (A. & C. Black), (2) *Studies in Education*.

A. Watson Bain, *The Modern Teacher* (Methuen).
 See chapters on History, Geography, and Citizenship.

Frederick J. Gould, *History the Teacher, Education inspired by Humanity's Story* (Methuen).

8. FREEDOM AND SELF-GOVERNMENT IN SCHOOLS.

Caldwell Cook, *The Play Way* (Macmillan).

J. H. Simpson, *An Adventure in Education* (Sidgwick & Jackson).

Homer Lane, *A Little Commonwealth*.

E. A. Craddock, *The Class Room Republic* (A. & C. Black).

Norman MacMunn, *A Path to Freedom in the School* (Bell).

Helen Parkhurst, *Education on the Dalton Plan* (Bell).

9. CIVICS (books suitable for use in schools).

Ernest F. Row, *Work, Wealth and Wages* (Harrap).

E. J. S. Lay, *Citizenship* (Macmillan), (Everyday Social Problems for the Nation's Youth).
 The best reader of its kind for upper standards of primary schools. The author has grasped the wide scope of the subject and presents its truths in a most interesting manner.

F. Swan, *A Primer of English Citizenship* (Longmans).
 The most comprehensive sketch of civics for school use. Contains useful questions and has been brought up to date.

E. R. Worts, *Citizenship*, New Teaching Series (Hodder & Stoughton).

Oscar Browning, *The Citizen; his Rights and Duties*.

Citizenship and the School

A. Williamson, *The Elements of Civics.*

E. Jenks, *The State and the Nation* (Dent).

C. H. Blakiston, *Elementary Civics.*
>   Adapted to the syllabus of the British Association Committee on Training in Citizenship. It is a simple and well-written outline.

C. H. Wyatt, *The English Citizen* (Longmans).

Richard Wilson, *The Complete Citizen* (Dent).
>   An introduction to civics based on history and literature and every-day life.

J. R. Peddie, *The British Citizen* (Blackie & Sons).
>   A book for young readers. Well illustrated and suitable for primary schools, but weak on economic side.

H. E. Malden, *The Rights and Duties of the English Citizen* (Methuen).

E. G. Houseley, *An Introductory Reader in Civics* (Harrap).

Sir T. Raleigh, *Elementary Politics* (Oxford Univ. Press).

MORE ADVANCED BOOKS.

Conrad Gill, *Government and People* (Methuen).

E. Jenks, *An Outline of English Local Government, The Government of the British Empire* (Murray).

J. A. R. Marriott, *English Political Institutions* (Oxford Univ. Press).

Lord Bryce, *The Hindrances to Good Citizenship* (Yale Univ. Press).

A. E. Duchesne, *Democracy and Empire* (Oxford Univ. Press).

DOCUMENTS.

Barnard, *Companion to English History in the Middle Ages**.

Bland, Brown, and Tawney, *English Economic History—Select Documents** (Bell).

A. & C. Black's Series of "English History Illustrated from Original Sources."

Keatinge and Frazer, *Documents of British History* (A. & C. Black), (with problems and exercises).

The Historical Association's *Constitutional Documents* (Bell).

Messrs Bell's Series of "English History Source Books."

C. W. Colby, *Selections from the Sources of English History** (Longmans).

Stubbs, *Select Charters**.

G. G. Coulton, *Social Life in Britain from the Conquest to the Reformation** (Cambridge Univ. Press).

R. B. Morgan, *Readings in English Social History* (Cambridge Univ. Press).

>   Books marked * suitable for school library.

INDEX

Administration, 21, 47, 57, 79, 121
Adolescence, 115
Adult education, 5
Adult suffrage, 1
Aims of teaching, 1, 29, 38, 41, 56, 59, 67, 71, 77, 105, 118, 120, 141
Aletaster, 93
Aliens, 45
American history, 34; independence, 113; taxation, 113
Aristotle, 50
Army, 16, 127
Artillery, 94
Assembly, in Athens, 43; in Rome, 53
Assize of Arms, 81
Assizes, 132
Average, citizen and schoolboy, 19, 20
Aviation, 122

'Balance,' in teaching, 32, 36, 140
Barbarians, 64
Barons, 79
Barter, 146
Burbryce, 74
Bureaucrats, 65
Burke, 113
Burleigh, 107

Cabinet, 9, 111, 121
Capital, 109, 142
Caput, 55
Ceremonies, 160
Charge to jury, 93
Charles II, 109
Citizens, 7; of Athens, 42; of Rome, 57
City State, 42, 53
Civic Education League, 8, 17

Civil actions, 81
Class room, 123
Clitheroe, 32, 90
Collaboration, 25, 26, 28, 145
Comites, 72
Commerce, 147, 149, 155
Common Law, 133
Communal responsibility, 38, 160
Communications, 65
Community, 69; feeling, 72, 168; life, 45
Comradeship, 89
Conduct marks, 65
Constable, 93
Constitution, 49, 56
Consuls, 57
Content, of civics, 17, 21 ff.
Control, 169
Co-operation, 74, 96
Courts, 21, 33, 74, 81, 91, 92, 96
Cribbing, 165
Crown, 88, 98, 102, 104
Culture subjects, 5
Curia Regis, 81
Curriculum, 6, 16, 20

Dalton Plan, 163
Debt, 102, 109, 110
Decline, of Athens, 52; of Rome, 64; of Russian trade, 150
Defence, in Athens, 47; in Rome, 57, 65; in Anglo-Saxon England, 73; in Middle Ages, 97; in nineteenth century, 121, 127
Democracy, 1, 32, 44
Despotism, 144
Dictator, 69
Discipline, 54, 160, 161, 165, 169
Disputes, in Athens, 47; in Rome, 62; in England, 75, 91

For EU product safety concerns, contact us at Calle de José Abascal, 56–1°, 28003 Madrid, Spain or eugpsr@cambridge.org.